DTLR
TRANSPORT
LOCAL GOVERNMENT
REGIONS

Manual to the Building Regulations

Third Edition 2001

M. J. Billington

London : The Stationery Office

600056642

Department of the Environment, Transport and the Regions
Eland House
Bressenden Place
London SW1E 5DU
Telephone 0207 944 3000
Internet service http://www.dtlr.gov.uk

Printed in Great Britain for The Stationery Office on material containing post-consumer waste 75% and ECF pulp 25%.
73124   C150   12/01   9385   9972

CONTENTS

Contents

CONTENTS

Introduction

If you intend to put up a new building in England or Wales, or extend or alter an existing building, or put an existing building to a different use, the Building Regulations will probably apply. The main purpose of the Regulations is to ensure the health and safety of people in or about buildings. They are also concerned with energy conservation and with making buildings more convenient and accessible for people with disabilities.

You may also be required to seek planning permission, licensing, and approval under local Acts, from the local authority. Some authorities operate a one-stop shop so the client only has to deal with one department.

This Manual is chiefly about 'the Building Regulations 2000' as amended, which are subsequently referred to simply as 'the Regulations'.

Section 1 tells you the kind of work to which the Regulations apply.

Section 2 describes the two alternative systems of building control: you may choose either the local authority or an approved inspector to supervise the work. If you choose the latter route the Building (Approved Inspectors etc) Regulations 2000 (as amended) are also relevant, and are subsequently referred to as the Approved Inspectors Regulations.

Section 3 contains information on how the requirements of the Regulations may be met and includes details of the courses of action open to you in the event of disagreement with your local authority or approved inspector. It also contains the Regulations (as amended) and their schedules set out in full on the left hand pages. The right hand pages explain the requirements of the Regulations and refer you to other documents which you might need to read and other legislation which may be relevant.

Section 4 gives a brief summary of some of the more commonly encountered legislation which also applies to building and site development.

Section 5 contains a list of supporting documents and related useful addresses.

All the guidance in this manual is informal. It should not be taken as an authoritative interpretation of the Regulations.

It should be noted that this Manual incorporates new Regulations and the 2002 editions of the Approved Documents in connection with Parts H (Drainage and waste disposal), J (Combustion appliances and fuel storage systems) and L (Conservation of fuel and power). However, these provisions and Approved Documents do not come into force until 1 April 2002.

How to use the Manual

1. This manual will enable you to find out about the Regulations and the system of building control in England and Wales.

2. On the following page you will find a Master Flow Chart. The diamond-shaped boxes ask questions and by following the arrows in the chart you will be led to rectangular boxes containing information which will lead you to other sections in the Manual.

3. The first three sections of this Manual all follow the same format. Each starts with a flow chart based on the same principles as the Master Flow Chart referred to above. These 'subsidiary' flow charts will direct you to other sections and paragraphs in the Manual where you will find additional information and further explanations about the Regulations and the control system.

4. Each section ends with a summary chart which can be used as a check sheet.

5. The actual text of the Regulations is contained in Section 3 immediately after the summary chart. The text appears on the left hand pages of the Manual and explanatory notes containing references to relevant information sources and legislation appear on the right hand pages opposite the Regulation text.

6. There may be other legislation which applies to your proposal in addition to or instead of the Regulations. You will find a selection of the more commonly encountered legislation in Section 4

Master Flow Chart – Building
Regulation Control Procedures

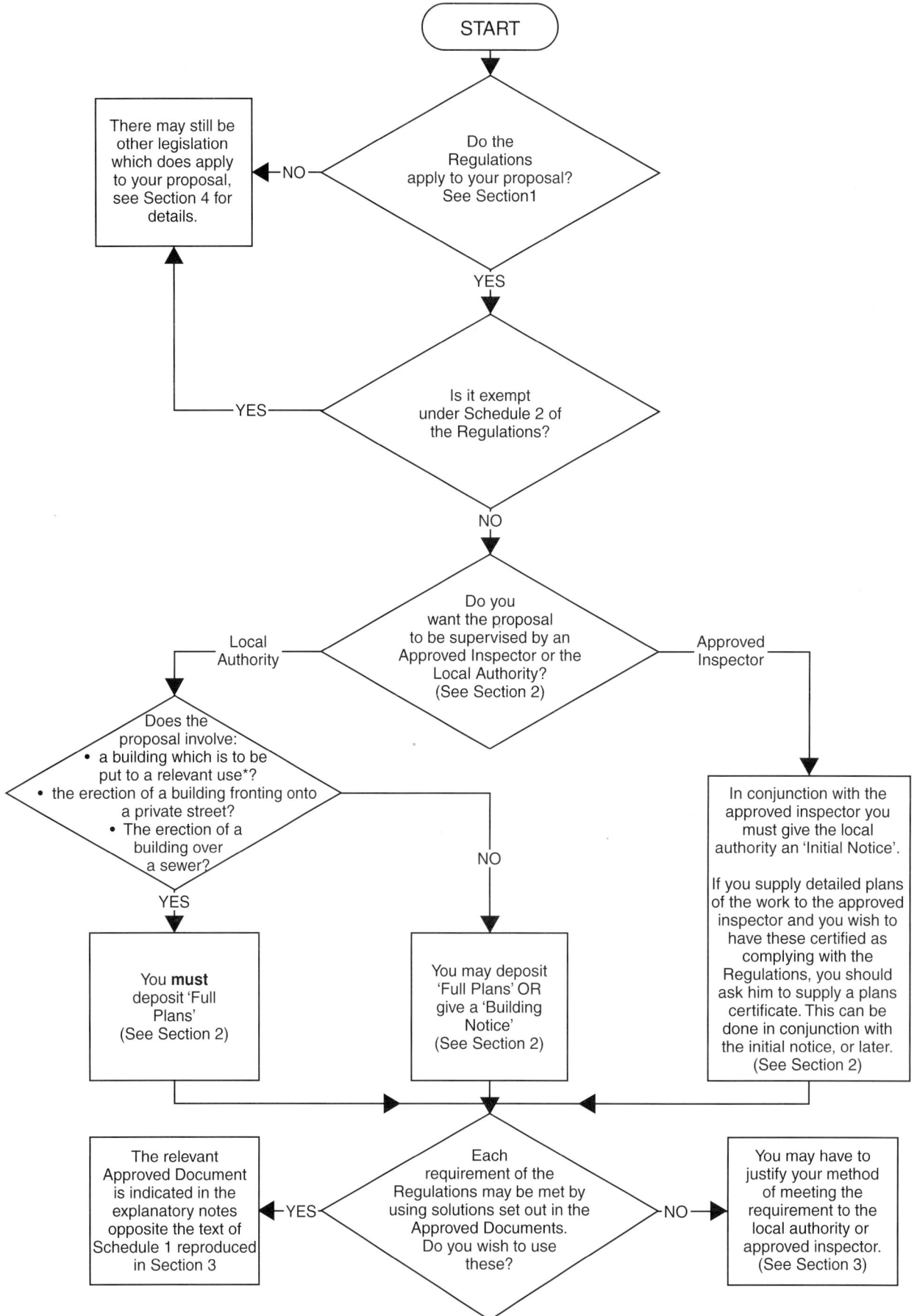

```
                              ┌──────────┐
                              │  START   │
                              └────┬─────┘
                                   ▼
```

START

Do the Regulations apply to your proposal? See Section1

NO → There may still be other legislation which does apply to your proposal, see Section 4 for details.

YES

Is it exempt under Schedule 2 of the Regulations?

YES → (to "There may still be other legislation..." box)

NO

Do you want the proposal to be supervised by an Approved Inspector or the Local Authority? (See Section 2)

Local Authority

Approved Inspector

Does the proposal involve:
- a building which is to be put to a relevant use*?
- the erection of a building fronting onto a private street?
- The erection of a building over a sewer?

YES

NO

You **must** deposit 'Full Plans' (See Section 2)

You may deposit 'Full Plans' OR give a 'Building Notice' (See Section 2)

In conjunction with the approved inspector you must give the local authority an 'Initial Notice'.

If you supply detailed plans of the work to the approved inspector and you wish to have these certified as complying with the Regulations, you should ask him to supply a plans certificate. This can be done in conjunction with the initial notice, or later. (See Section 2)

Each requirement of the Regulations may be met by using solutions set out in the Approved Documents. Do you wish to use these?

YES → The relevant Approved Document is indicated in the explanatory notes opposite the text of Schedule 1 reproduced in Section 3

NO → You may have to justify your method of meeting the requirement to the local authority or approved inspector. (See Section 3)

* 'relevant use' means a workplace of a kind to which Part II of the Fire Precautions (Workplace) Regulations 1997 (as amended by the Fire Precautions (Workplace) (Amendment) Regulations 1999) applies or a use designated under section 1 of the Fire Precautions Act 1971.

Section 1

DO THE BUILDING REGULATIONS APPLY TO YOUR PROPOSAL?

Contents

Flow Chart

```
                              ┌──────────┐
                              │  START   │
                              └──────────┘
                                    │
                                    ▼
                        Does the proposal involve
                                 work to:
                            • a Crown building,
          YES        • a school or other educational building[1],        NO
                • a building belonging to a statutory undertaker[2],
                        the UK Atomic Energy Authority,
                           or the Civil Aviation
                                 Authority.
```

It is possible that any work to such a building may **not** need to comply with the Building Regulations. Check with the local authority and see Paragraph 1.2 for more information[1].

NO

Does the proposal involve any of the building work items listed in the **YES** column in Section1 Summary Chart on page 11.

It is most likely that the Building Regulations will not apply to your proposal.

YES

There may be other legislation which does apply. See Section 4 for details.

As a general rule the Building Regulations **will** apply to your proposal, but there are exceptions. See the **NO** column in Section 1 Summary Chart on page 11.

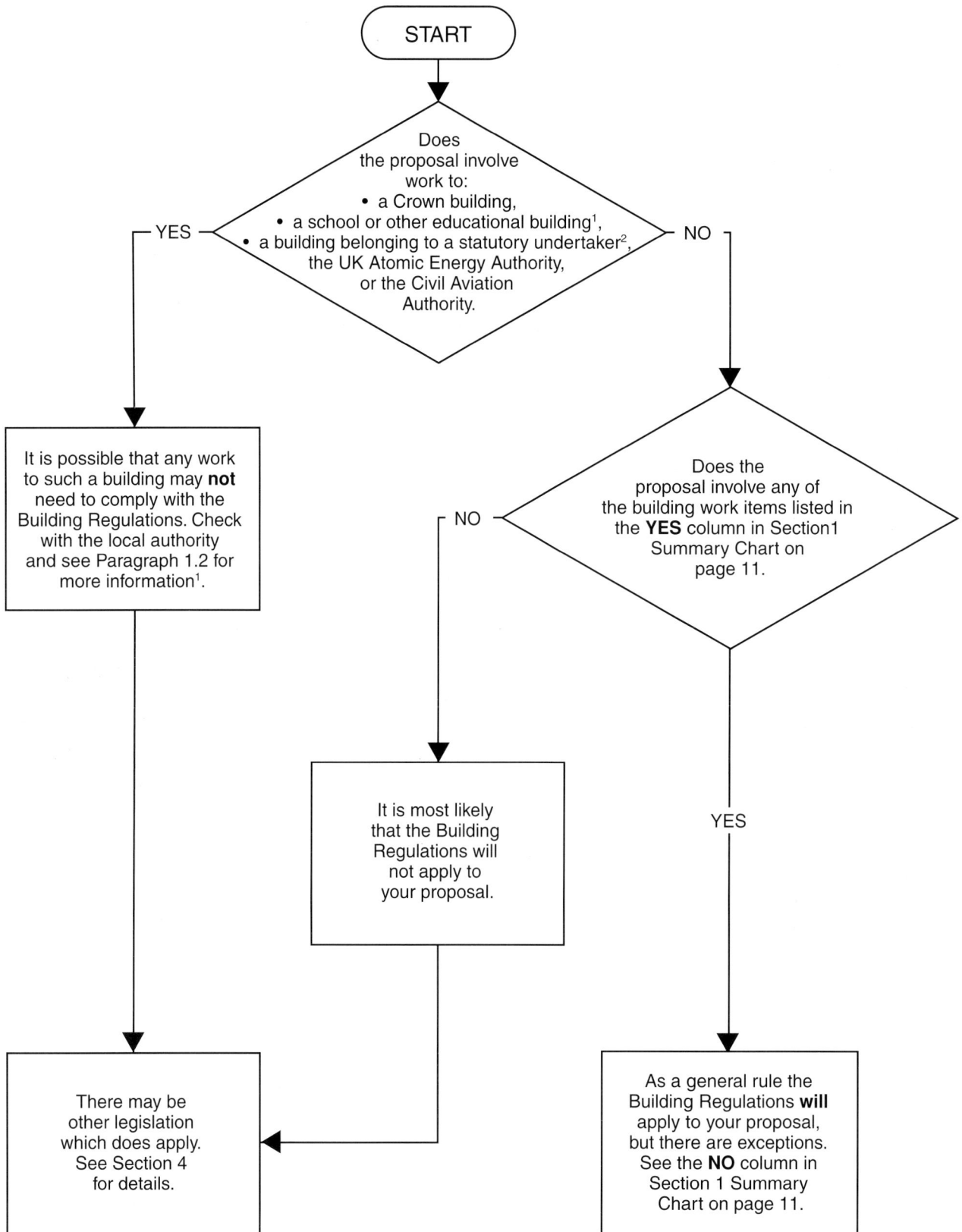

[1] By virtue of the Education (Schools and Further and Higher Education) (Amendment) (England) Regulations 2001, by 1 April 2001, all schools and further and higher education buildings in England are no longer exempt from the provisions of the Building Regulations 2000. It is anticipated that schools in Wales will lose their exemption in 2002.

[2] Regarding statutory undertakers, the fact that many former public bodies are now in private hands has meant that both gas and electricity suppliers are not now regarded as statutory undertakers under the Act. Additionally, the passing of the Postal Services Act 2000 has meant that Post Offices (including other universal providers of postal services) are no longer regarded as statutory undertakers.

Introduction

1.1 The Building Act 1984 and Regulations made under it apply to building work in England and Wales (Scotland and Northern Ireland have different legal frameworks*). However, building work carried out to Crown buildings (such as Government offices and courts of law) is not subject to control under the Regulations and the same may be true of certain other premises referred to the paragraphs 1.2 and 1.3 below.

Educational buildings and statutory undertakers

1.2 As a result of the repeal of Regulation 8 of the Education (Schools and Further and Higher Education) Regulations (SI 1989/351), schools in England are no longer exempt from the Building Regulations. The Department for Education and Skills has issued guidance on constructional standards for schools[†], indicating where it is necessary to supplement the Approved Documents to take account of the specific requirements of schools. It is proposed that in due course the Approved Documents will be amended to take account of these. Further information on this can be obtained from the School Premises Team, Department for Education and Skills, Caxton House, Room 762, 6 – 12 Tothill Street, London SW1H 9NA, Tel 020 7273 6023, E-mail: premises.schools@dfes.gsi.gov.uk. It is expected that schools in Wales will lose their exemption in early 2002.

Under section 4 of the Building Act 1984, a building belonging to statutory undertakers (as defined in section 126 Building Act 1984), the United Kingdom Atomic Energy Authority, or the Civil Aviation Authority is exempt from the application of building regulations, provided that the building in question is held or used by them for the purposes of their undertaking. However, this exemption is subject to the following exceptions, in respect of which building regulations do apply:

i)   a house;

ii)   a building used as offices or showrooms unless:

    a)   it forms part of a railway station, or

    b)   in the case of the Civil Aviation Authority, it is on an aerodrome owned by the Authority.

A further class which enjoys an exemption under section 4 is "relevant airport operators" as defined in section 57 of the Airports Act 1986. Section 4 applies in relation to a relevant airport operator as it applies to a statutory undertaker, subject to the following variations:

i)   hotels are excluded from the benefit of the section 4 exemption;

ii)   offices and showrooms enjoy the benefit of the section 4 exemption, if they are on any airport to which Part V of the Airport Act 1986 applies.

Additionally, the fact that many former public bodies are now in private hands has meant that both gas and electricity suppliers are not now regarded as statutory undertakers under section 4 of the Building Act 1984. Furthermore, it should be noted that the Post Office lost its statutory undertaker status in relation to building regulations, in March 2001[**].

Other exempt bodies

1.3 Using the powers available under Section 5 of the Building Act 1984, The Metropolitan Police Authority has been exempted from having to comply with the procedural requirements of building control, although it is still required to comply with the substantive or technical requirements of the Regulations.[***] As an exempt body the Metropolitan Police Authority is also exempt from the enforcement procedures by local authorities.

Building work

1.4 Building work is defined in Regulation 3(1) as:

(i)   the erection or extension of a building,

(ii)   subject to Regulation 3(1A), the provision or extension of a controlled service or fitting in or in connection with a building,

(iii)   the material alteration of a building, or a controlled service or fitting[‡] under the circumstances given in Regulation 3(2),

(iv)   work required by Regulation 6 in connection with a material change of use,

(v)   the insertion of insulation into the cavity wall of a building,

(vi)   work involving the underpinning of a building,

Under the terms of Regulation 3(1A), the provision of a controlled service or fitting in an existing dwelling is not building work if the service or fitting is "controlled" only because

---

* For Scotland see The Building Standards (Scotland) Regulations 1990 (as amended) and for Northern Ireland see The Building Regulations (Northern Ireland) 1994 (as amended).
† Guidance on the Constructional Standards for Schools: DfES 142/2001-09-11
** The Postal Services Act 2001 (Consequential Modifications No. 1) Order 2001.
***The Building Regulations (Amendment) Regulations 2000 (SI 2000 No. 1554).
‡ See pp 30 and 32 for the definition of controlled service or fitting.

Part L1 imposes requirements in relation to it, *unless* the service or fitting is:

- a window, rooflight or roof window,

- a door (which together with its frame has more than 50 per cent of its internal face area glazed),

- a space heating or hot water service boiler, or

- a hot water vessel,

is regarded as building work in its own right with regard to the provisions of Part L (Conservation of fuel and power).

Exempt buildings

1.5 Certain small buildings and extensions as well as buildings used for special purposes are entirely exempt under the Regulations. You can find them listed in Schedule 2 to the Regulations (see pages 84 to 87 in this Manual.)

Repairs and alterations

1.6 Works of repair are not normally covered by the Regulations. Repair is not defined in the Regulations, but is usually taken to mean replacement, redecoration, routine maintenance, making good, but not new work or alteration. However, replacement of a controlled service or fitting is regarded as provision of such a service or fitting, and is therefore building work. The replacement of, for example, complete windows, even if they are fitted into the original openings without altering the structure of the building, is now building work and so subject to the Regulations. Windows, rooflights, roof windows and doors are taken to include the fixed frame as well as the moving elements. This means that only the provision of complete new window or door installations (as distinct from (e.g.) repairs to the moving part of a window) is provision of a controlled fitting.

If you are in doubt about whether or not your work is covered by the Regulations, the local authority (or an approved inspector) may be able to advise you.

1.7 Alterations (as distinct from extensions) to existing buildings and to controlled services and fittings are not controlled unless they fall under the definition of material alteration contained in Regulation 3(2). Alterations are considered to be material if they would affect compliance with the following requirements of Schedule 1 at any stage of the work:

Part A (structure)

paragraph B1 (means of warning and escape)

paragraph B3 (internal fire spread – structure)

paragraph B4 (external fire spread)

paragraph B5 (access and facilities for the fire service)

Part M (access and facilities for disabled people).

For example, re-covering of roofs with tiles of a similar mass to the original tiles is not covered by the Regulations, but the use of tiles which are heavier or lighter than the originals may have structural implications and so is controlled as a material alteration (see Approved Document to Part A, Section 3).

Compliance

1.8 Regulation 4(1) states that on completion, the building work should:

a) comply with the relevant requirements contained in Schedule 1, and

b) not adversely affect compliance with other requirements.

For example, a new internal wall should comply with the requirements for walls, and it should not obstruct airflow necessary to satisfy the requirements for ventilation.

Regulation 4(2) requires that after building work has been completed, extended or altered buildings and controlled services should still comply with the relevant requirements of Schedule 1 or where they did not comply before, the situation should not be any worse on completion.

Change of use

1.9 Not every change of use of a building is subject to the Regulations. Those that are covered are termed *material changes of use* (as defined in Regulation 5) and are those where:

(a) the building is used as a dwelling, hotel, boarding house, institution or public building* where previously it was not, or

(b) the building contains a flat where previously it did not, or

(c) the building is no longer exempt under Schedule 2 where previously it was, or

(d) a building containing at least one dwelling is converted to provide a greater or lesser number of dwellings than it did previously. The term dwelling includes a flat.

The requirements relating to a material change of use are given in Regulation 6 (see page 36).

---

* Public building is defined in Regulation 2(2) see page 32. Institution has a special meaning under the Regulations (see Regulation 2(1), page 32)

DO THE BUILDING REGULATIONS APPLY TO YOUR PROPOSAL?

Summary Chart

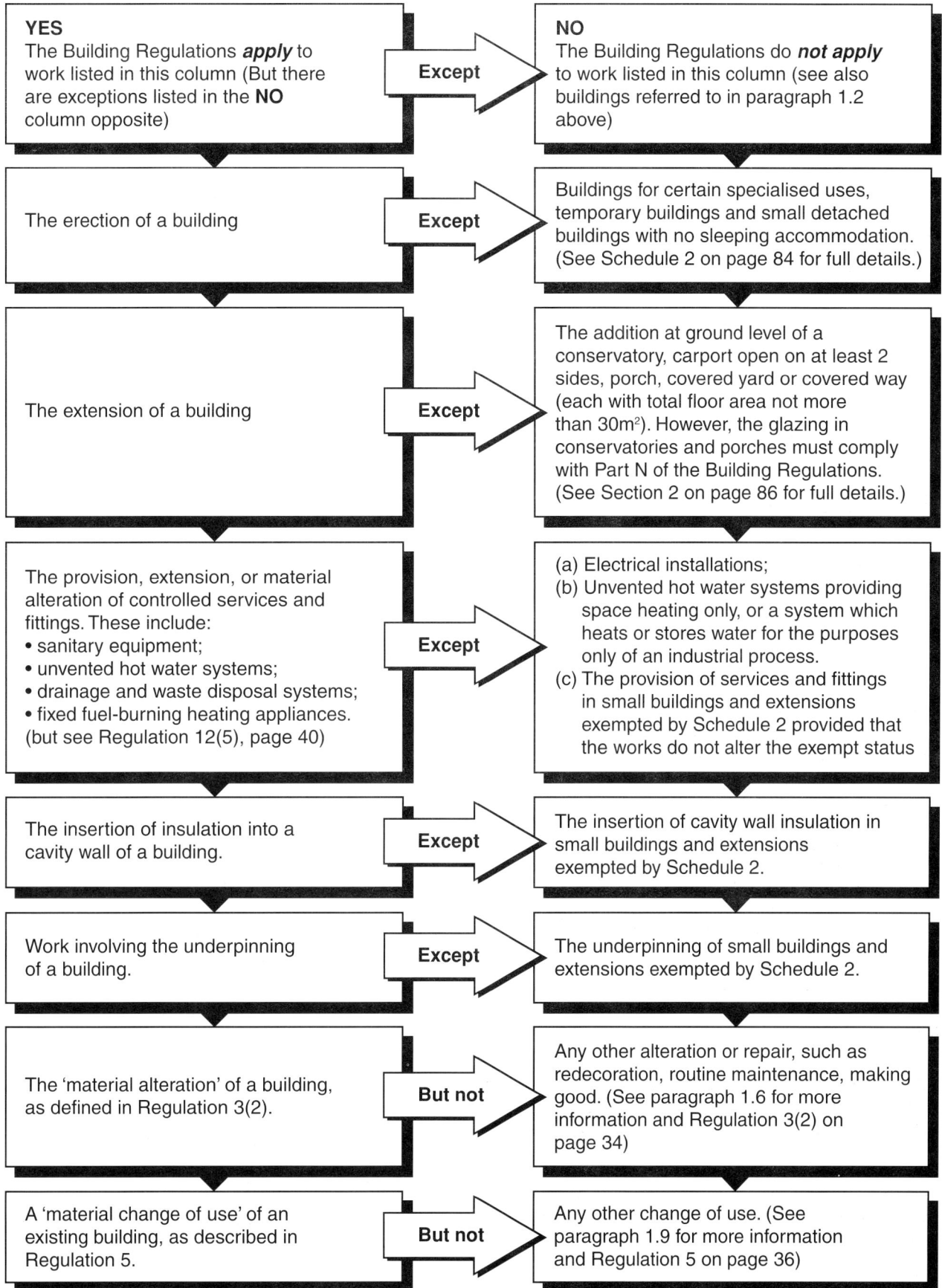

YES		NO
YES The Building Regulations *apply* to work listed in this column (But there are exceptions listed in the **NO** column opposite)	**Except** ➤	**NO** The Building Regulations do *not apply* to work listed in this column (see also buildings referred to in paragraph 1.2 above)
The erection of a building	**Except** ➤	Buildings for certain specialised uses, temporary buildings and small detached buildings with no sleeping accommodation. (See Schedule 2 on page 84 for full details.)
The extension of a building	**Except** ➤	The addition at ground level of a conservatory, carport open on at least 2 sides, porch, covered yard or covered way (each with total floor area not more than 30m²). However, the glazing in conservatories and porches must comply with Part N of the Building Regulations. (See Section 2 on page 86 for full details.)
The provision, extension, or material alteration of controlled services and fittings. These include: • sanitary equipment; • unvented hot water systems; • drainage and waste disposal systems; • fixed fuel-burning heating appliances. (but see Regulation 12(5), page 40)	**Except** ➤	(a) Electrical installations; (b) Unvented hot water systems providing space heating only, or a system which heats or stores water for the purposes only of an industrial process. (c) The provision of services and fittings in small buildings and extensions exempted by Schedule 2 provided that the works do not alter the exempt status
The insertion of insulation into a cavity wall of a building.	**Except** ➤	The insertion of cavity wall insulation in small buildings and extensions exempted by Schedule 2.
Work involving the underpinning of a building.	**Except** ➤	The underpinning of small buildings and extensions exempted by Schedule 2.
The 'material alteration' of a building, as defined in Regulation 3(2).	**But not** ➤	Any other alteration or repair, such as redecoration, routine maintenance, making good. (See paragraph 1.6 for more information and Regulation 3(2) on page 34)
A 'material change of use' of an existing building, as described in Regulation 5.	**But not** ➤	Any other change of use. (See paragraph 1.9 for more information and Regulation 5 on page 36)

Manual to the Building Regulations   Do the Building Regulations apply to your proposal?

11

Section 2

THE TWO SYSTEMS OF BUILDING CONTROL

Contents

Flow Chart

START

Do you want the proposal to be checked by an Approved Inspector or the Local Authority?

Approved Inspector

Local Authority

NO

Does the proposal involve:
- a building which is to be put to a relevant use[1]?
- the erection of a building fronting onto a private street?
- the erection of a building over a sewer?

YES

Agree contract terms including arranging for payment of approved inspector's fee (this is negotiable) and whether you require a plans certificate[2].

In conjuction with the approved inspector you must give the local authority an '**Initial Notice**'[3].

You may deposit 'Full Plans' OR give a 'Building Notice'.

You **must** deposit 'Full Plans'.

Full Plans

Building Notice

Agree conditions regarding giving notice of commencement and of certain other stages of work with approved inspector.

Local authority must accept or reject initial notice within 5 days[5].

Deposit Building Notice and pay charge[4].

Deposit Full Plans and pay plan charge.

Start work.

You may start work after giving local authority at least 2 clear working days notice.

You may start work after giving local authority at least 2 clear working days notice[6]. Pay inspection charge.

Local authority must pass or reject plans within 5 weeks, or if you agree, 2 months[7].

You must comply with the Regulations. Your approved inspector will give you a written notice if he considers that the work contravenes the Regulations. Failure to remedy the contravention within 3 months of such a notice will lead to cancellation of the initial notice by the approved inspector.[8]

Provide additional plans and details if requested by local authority.

You **must** notify the local authority at certain stages during the work. (see Regulation 15)

When the work is complete to the satisfaction of the approved inspector he will give a **final certificate** to the local authority.

Provided the local authority are satisfied that the work complies with the Regulation they will under certain circumstances[9], give you a **completion certificate**.

You **must** comply with the Regulations or the local authority may serve a notice on you requiring you to take down or alter any work which they consider to be in contravention. If you do not accept their view you may challenge it.

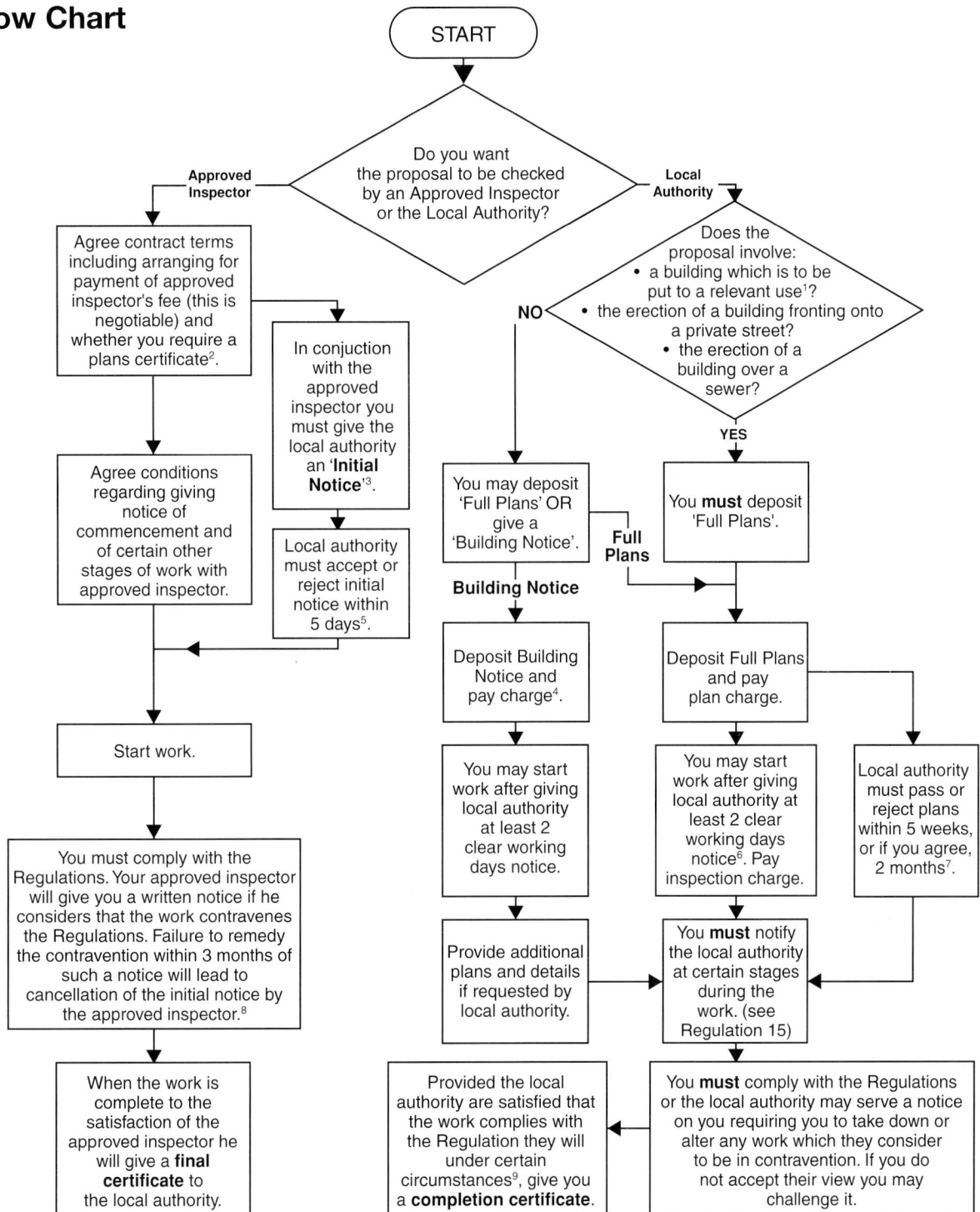

1 'relevant use' means a workplace of a kind to which Part II of the Fire Precautions (Workplace) Regulations 1997 (as amended by the Fire Precautions (Workplace) (Amendment) Regulations 1999) applies or a use designated under section 1 of the Fire Precautions Act 1971 (these include hotels, boarding houses, offices, shops, railway premises and factories).

2 A plans certificate may be combined with the initial notice or given subsequently.

3 An initial notice must be accompanied by certain details and by evidence that the approved inspector is suitably insured. You may also request that your approved inspector supply you and the local authority with a plans certificate.

4 The charge payable is equivalent to the sum total of the plan charge and the inspection charge and is payable in one instalment when the notice is deposited.

5 You should not start work before the initial notice has been accepted by the local authority, or 5 days have passed without it being rejected, when it will be presumed to have been accepted. You should not start work if the notice is rejected.

6 If the local authority reject your plans or the approved inspector is unable to give a plans certificate you may ask the Secretary for Transport, Local Government and the Regions, or the National Assembly of Wales for a determination. A fee is payable.

7 You are not required to wait for the plans to be passed before starting work, but if you proceed without approval, you do so at your own risk (see 2.12).

8 If the initial notice is cancelled you must not continue with the work unless it is being supervised either by a new approved inspector or by the local authority. You may engage another approved inspector unless the local authority has taken positive steps to supervise the work.

9 The local authority will give you a completion certificate if the work affects a building which is subject to a relevant use or you requested a certificate when you made a full plans submission.

Introduction

2.1 You must first decide whether you want the local authority to provide the building control service or whether you wish to employ an approved inspector. Local authorities are able to provide a building control service for all categories of work and for any building type. They may also be responsible for other statutory requirements e.g. licensing, which may affect the design of the building. However, you will not have a contractual arrangement with the local authority.

Approved inspectors are private sector companies or individuals, authorised under the Building Act to provide a building control service for all categories of work and for any building type. However not all approved inspectors currently have insurance cover enabling them to take on the inspection of all descriptions of building work. (Section 5 of this manual tells you where to get more information about approved inspectors currently approved). You will have a formal contractual arrangement with your approved inspector and you will be able to negotiate fees. Except for defined minor work, approved inspectors must be financially and professionally independent of the work they inspect (see 2.21).

LOCAL AUTHORITY CONTROL

2.2 If you decide on the local authority you may have a further choice of depositing full plans or giving them a building notice, which contains much less information. To start work without doing either is a contravention of Regulation 12 for which the local authority can prosecute. In either case you will have to pay the required charge (see Section 4, paragraph 4.15).

2.3 Before deciding whether to deposit full plans or give a building notice you should consider the differences between the two procedures which are explained in the following paragraphs. If you are proposing to erect or carry out building work to a building which is already put (or will be put) to a 'relevant use', you must deposit full plans (see paragraph 2.9 and Regulation 12 on page 38). A 'relevant use' means a use as a workplace of a kind to which Part II of the Fire Precautions (Workplace) Regulations 1997* applies or a use designated under section 1 of the Fire Precautions Act 1971. Currently designated are hotels, boarding houses, offices, shops, railway premises and factories.

You must also deposit full plans if you propose to:

- carry out work which includes the erection of a building fronting onto a private street, or

- carry out building work which involves building over a sewer. This is to allow consultation to take place with the sewerage undertaker under the provisions of regulation 14A (see paragraph 2.10 below).

Deposit of plans

2.4 If you deposit 'full plans' (defined in Regulation 14) the local authority must pass or reject them within 5 weeks, or 2 months if you agree to this in writing[†]. You must also pay the 'plan charge'. The local authority can reject the plans on any of the following grounds (which must be given in the notice of rejection):

a) the plans show a contravention of the Regulations;

b) the plans are defective (e.g. incomplete – they fail to show compliance with the Regulations);

c) they are unsatisfactory as regards the local authority's functions under s. 25 of the Building Act.

d) they fail to show compliance with relevant local Acts.

The 'linked powers'

2.5 The functions referred to in paragraph 2.4(c) are usually referred to as the 'linked powers' because their operation is linked to the deposit of plans. Most of these functions have been replaced by Building Regulations, the most recent being ss 18 and 21 of the Building Act which will be substantially replaced by Regulations H1 and H4 respectively with the coming into force of the first amendment[‡]. The only remaining linked power is Section 25, which enables a local authority to insist on the provision of a wholesome water supply to houses.

Local Acts of Parliament

2.6 Local Acts of Parliament exist in some areas enabling local authorities to reject plans on particular grounds, although the need for much of this local legislation is currently under review. (See Section 4, paragraph 4.9 for more information on local legislation).

Building in accordance with plans

2.7 You are not obliged under the Regulations to build exactly in conformity with the plans which you deposited – your obligation is to see that the work complies with the requirements of the Regulations. Nevertheless, where you have

---

* as amended by the Fire Precautions (Workplace) (Amendment) Regulations 1999 SI 1999/1877
† See also the Building Act 1984, sec. 16.
‡ The Building (Amendment) Regulations 2001 SI 2001/3335 coming into force 1 April 2002.

had your plans passed (or they were not rejected) and the work conforms with them, you gain useful protection because the local authority may not then serve a notice requiring you to take it down or alter it (see paragraph 2.13). If you propose to deviate significantly from the approved plans, you are advised to consult the local authority first.

The building notice

2.8 If you decide to give a building notice, you must include in it a site plan (in the case of a new building or extension) and the information specified in Regulation 13. This is to enable the local authority to identify the site or the property concerned, the nature of the work proposed, and also to consider any aspect of the work to which local legislation might relate. You will also need to pay the required charge. This is equivalent to the sum of the plan charge and the inspection charge and is payable in one instalment when the notice is given

The local authority may ask you to provide certain other plans or information, but there is no requirement for it to pass or reject a building notice or any such plans which you provide. Consequently, the protection of having had your plans passed is not available. There is also no procedure to seek a determination from the Secretary of State if there is a disagreement between you and the local authority – unless plans are subsequently deposited (see 3.14).

The local authority can require work to be altered if it is not satisfactory in respect of matters covered by the linked powers, but see paragraph 2.5 above, just as it can if work contravenes the Regulations. On the other hand the building notice enables you to start work without having to provide the local authority with plans. You must however inform the local authority before you start the work (see paragraph 2.12). Under Regulation 13(7), a building notice will cease to have effect if the work has not started within three years.

Consulting the fire authority

2.9 If you are proposing to erect a building which will be put to a relevant use you are obliged to deposit full plans so that the local authority can consult the fire authority. (See Regulation 12(3)). This is necessary since, in many cases, a fire certificate will be required under the Fire Precautions Act when the building is eventually used and this is obtained by application to the local fire authority.

Details of the consultation procedures which should be followed at the design and construction stages of a contract are given in the publication *Building Regulations and Fire Safety Procedural Guidance*, issued jointly by the Home Office, the National Assembly for Wales and the DTLR, in February 2001.

Consultations with the sewerage undertaker

2.10 If you intend to erect, extend or carry out underpinning works to a building within 3m of the centreline of a drain, sewer or disposal main which is shown on any map of sewers kept by the sewerage undertaker under s 199 of the Water Industry Act 1991 you must deposit full plans with the local authority. This is to enable the local authority to carry out its duties under Regulation 14A to consult the sewerage undertaker as soon as practicable after the plans have been deposited. The local authority is not permitted to pass the plans or issue a completion certificate until the consultation has taken place (the sewerage undertaker has up to 15 days to reply) and it must have regard to the views expressed by the sewerage undertaker. The local authority must be satisfied that the work will be carried out in a way that is not detrimental to the building or extension or to the continued maintenance of the drain, sewer or disposal main.

Conditional passing of plans

2.11 There is an alternative to giving a building notice or depositing full plans at the outset. Section 16(2) of the Building Act allows a local authority to pass plans subject to either or both of the following conditions:

a)   that such modifications as the local authority may specify shall be made in the deposited plans. This means that where the plans are incomplete or show a contravention the local authority may pass them subject to the necessary additions or amendments being made;

b)   that such further plans as the local authority may specify shall be deposited. This means that if the plans are incomplete it may pass them subject to the remainder being deposited. This second condition enables plans to be dealt with in stages.

These procedures can often be useful, though local authorities are not obliged to use them and your written agreement is required.

Starting work and giving notices at certain stages

2.12 If you have decided to serve a Building Notice you may begin work at any time, provided that you give the LA two clear working days notice of commencement as required by Regulation 15(1)(a). On the other hand, if you have opted to deposit a full plans application you should wait for a notice of approval from the LA. Once you have approval you may begin work providing again, you give the LA two clear working days notice of commencement. If you proceed with your work after depositing full plans but before receiving approval, you do so at your own risk because the LA will be entitled to use its enforcement powers under section 36 of the Building Act 1984.

Apart from requiring you to give notice of commencement to the LA, Regulation 15 also requires you to notify the LA when you have reached various stages of the work and specifies the relevant time periods within which this must be done. Failure to comply with Regulation 15 in this respect will put you in breach of the regulations; and under Regulation 15 the LA is empowered to require by notice the opening up or pulling down of any work the compliance of which they are uncertain.

Contravention of the technical requirements

2.13 If during the course of the building work, or within a year of completion, the local authority considers that your work contravenes any requirement of the Regulations it may serve a notice (under section 36 of the Building Act) requiring you to take down or alter the work within 28 days. If you disagree with the views of the local authority you may notify the it that you propose to obtain an independent expert report under section 37, in which case the period is extended to 70 days. The local authority may withdraw the notice in the light of the report, but if it does not you may appeal to the magistrate's court under section 40. It should be noted that if you use the approved inspector system, the local authority cannot give a section 36 notice in relation to any work described in an initial notice, so long as it remains in force, or in a final certificate which has been accepted.

Energy rating

2.14 If you intend to erect a dwelling (or change the use of a building so that it becomes a dwelling) its energy rating must be calculated by the standard assessment procedure (SAP). Notice of the energy rating must be given to the local authority not more than 5 days after the work has been completed. If the dwelling is occupied before completion, notice of the energy rating must be given to the local authority, not less than 5 days before occupation.

Unless you intend to occupy the dwelling yourself, you must affix a notice which states the calculated energy rating of the dwelling in a conspicuous place in the dwelling. In DETR Circular 07/2000 the Department suggested that the notice should be typed on A4 paper and placed in a suitable plastic holder for protection. It should be double-sided and should be attached by non-marking adhesive to a window near, or in, the front door. In flats

(where there is no suitable window in or near the front door) it could be fixed to a sitting room or kitchen window.

The time periods for fixing the notice are identical to those for notifying the local authority above.

Completion certificates

2.15 Where Full Plans are submitted for work to a building which is put (or is intended to be put) to a relevant use (see paragraph 2.3) the local authority must issue you with a Completion Certificate about compliance with the fire safety requirements of the Building Regulations once work has finished. In other circumstances, you may ask to be given one when the work is finished, but you must make your request when you first submit your plans. In this case the completion certificate will relate to any parts of the Regulations which are applicable to the work.

Duration of approval

2.16 If you have had full plans passed by the local authority and you do not commence the work within 3 years of the date on which the plans were passed, the local authority may serve a notice on you under s.32 of the Building Act, rescinding the approval of plans.

BUILDING CONTROL BY APPROVED INSPECTORS*

The initial notice

2.17 If you engage an approved inspector you and the inspector must jointly give to the local authority an initial notice which must be accompanied by a declaration signed by the insurer, that an approved scheme of insurance applies to the work. (See the Approved Inspectors Regulations, Regulation 8).

There is a prescribed form for an initial notice (see form 1 in schedule 2 to the Approved Inspectors Regulations). The notice must contain:

a)   a description of the work;

b)   in the case of a new building or extension:

   (i)   a site plan to a scale of not less than 1:1250 showing the boundaries and location of the site;

   (ii)   a statement that the approved inspector will consult the sewerage undertaker where the work involves building over or near any drain, sewer or disposal main which is shown on any map of sewers kept by the sewerage undertaker;

---

* See the Building Act 1984, sections 47 to 58 (as amended) and the Building (Approved Inspectors etc.) Regulations 2000 (as amended)

THE TWO SYSTEMS OF BUILDING CONTROL

(iii)   a statement of any local legislation relevant to the work and the steps to be taken to comply with it. See section 4, paragraph 4.9 below for more information on local legislation.

The local authority needs to know whether drainage will be connected to an existing sewer. For this purpose, it will often be sufficient to indicate that the connection will be between points A and B on the plan. Where it is not proposed to connect to an existing sewer, the initial notice must include a statement as to how drainage discharges are to be dealt with. For example, this could include details of the location of any septic tank and associated secondary treatment system, or any wastewater treatment system or cesspool.

Where the work described in the initial notice relates to a building, which is to be put to a relevant use, the notice must contain a declaration that the approved inspector will consult the fire authority before giving a plans certificate or final certificate (see paragraphs 2.22).

Acceptance and rejection of initial notice

2.18 You should ensure that all the required information is provided in the prescribed form, because if the local authority is not satisfied that the notice contains sufficient information, it must reject the initial notice. The local authority has 5 working days in which to consider the notice and may only reject it on prescribed grounds*. Because of the short time scales involved, it is important that the initial notice is addressed to the correct part of the local authority and the correct building.

If the local authority does not reject the initial notice within 5 working days (beginning on the day the notice is given to the local authority) it is presumed to have accepted the initial notice unconditionally.

2.19 Once the notice has been accepted, or is deemed to have been accepted by the passing of five days, the approved inspector is responsible for supervising the work as regards:

(i)   compliance with Regulations 4, 6 and 7 of the Building Regulations;

(ii)   compliance, where relevant, with Regulation 12 of the Approved Inspectors Regulations concerning the calculation of energy ratings for dwellings.

Independence of approved inspectors

2.20 The approved inspector must have no professional or financial interest in the work he supervises.[†] Essentially, this means that he must be independent of the designer, builder or owner, unless the work is minor work.

This is defined as:-

a)   the material alteration or extension of a one or two storey house, provided that the house has no more than three storeys on completion of the work;

b)   the provision, extension or material alteration of a controlled service or fitting in any building;

c)   work consisting of the underpinning of any building.

Consulting the fire authority

2.21 If you are proposing to erect, extend, carry out a material alteration to, or change the use of, a building which will be put to (or will continue to be put to) a relevant use, the approved inspector is required, to consult the fire authority.

The consultation must take place at the following stages:

(a)   before or as soon as is practicable after giving an initial notice or an amendment notice (see paragraph 2.33);

(b)   before giving a plans certificate (whether or not this is combined with an initial notice); and

(c)   before giving a final certificate.

In the case of (a) above, the approved inspector must supply the fire authority with sufficient plans to show that the work described in the initial notice will comply with Part B of Schedule 1. In the case of (b) above, he must supply the fire authority with a copy of the plans in relation to which he intends to give the plans certificate. Additionally, he must allow the fire authority up to 15 working days to comment, and have regard to the views it expresses, before giving a plans certificate (see paragraph 2.24) or final certificate (see paragraph 2.26) to the local authority[‡].

Consultations with the sewerage undertaker

2.22 Where an initial notice or amendment notice is to be given (or has been given) and you intend to erect, extend or carry out underpinning works to a building within 3m of the centreline of a drain, sewer or disposal

---

* See Schedule 3 to the Building (Approved Inspectors etc.) Regulations 2000 as amended)
† See Regulation 10 of the Building (Approved Inspectors etc.) Regulations 2000 (as amended)
‡ See Regulation 13 of the Building (Approved Inspectors etc.) Regulations 2000. (as amended)

main to which paragraph H4 of Schedule 1 applies, the approved inspector must consult the sewerage undertaker. The procedures and time periods involved parallel those described for fire authority consultations (see paragraph 2.22).

Plans certificate

2.23 If you wish to have detailed plans of the work (or a part of it) certified as complying with the Regulations, you should ask your approved inspector to supply a plans certificate. If he is satisfied with the plans he must give a plans certificate to you and the local authority (Approved Inspectors Regulations 14 to 16 and the Building Act s.50). This can be done at the time the initial notice is given, or later. Possession of a plans certificate can give you valuable protection in the event that the initial notice is cancelled or ceases to be in force and no new initial notice is given or accepted (see paragraph 2.30).

Energy rating

2.24 If you intend to erect a dwelling (or change the use of a building so that it becomes a dwelling) its energy rating must be calculated by the standard assessment procedure (SAP). Notice of the energy rating must be given to the approved inspector who gave the initial notice not more than 5 days after the work has been completed. If the dwelling is occupied before completion, notice of the energy rating must be given to the approved inspector, not more than 8 weeks after the date of occupation. In the case of a dwelling created by a material change of use, notice of the energy rating must be given to the approved inspector, not more than 8 weeks after the date on which the change of use takes place.

Unless you intend to occupy the dwelling yourself, you must affix a notice which states the calculated energy rating of the dwelling, in a conspicuous place in the dwelling. In DETR Circular 07/2000 the Department suggested that the notice should be typed on A4 paper and placed in a suitable plastic holder for protection. It should be double-sided and should be attached by non-marking adhesive to a window near, or in, the front door. In flats (where there is no suitable window in or near the front door) it could be fixed to a sitting room or kitchen window.

The time periods for fixing the notice are identical to those for notifying the approved inspector above.

Final certificate

2.25 When the work is complete the approved inspector must give the local authority a final certificate (Approved Inspectors Regulation 17 and the Building Act s. 51). The local authority

may reject this only on the prescribed grounds given in Schedule 5 to the Approved Inspectors Regulations, and they must do this within 10 working days. If a final certificate is rejected the initial notice ceases to be in force on the expiry of four weeks beginning with the day on which the rejection is given (see also paragraph 2.30).

As in the case of a plans certificate, a final certificate need not relate to all the work specified in an initial notice. For example, where a single initial notice covered a new housing estate, separate final or plans certificates might be given for individual houses or groups of houses.

Occupation etc.

2.26 Where an initial notice is given for the erection, extension or material alteration of a building and the building or extension or any part which has been materially altered is subsequently occupied and no final certificate is given, the initial notice will cease to have effect.

For most buildings there is a period of grace of 8 weeks from the date of occupation before the initial notice lapses, but in the case of a building to be put to a relevant use the period is four weeks.

Similarly, if the initial notice relates to a material change of use and no final certificate is given and the change of use takes place, the initial notice will cease to have effect eight weeks after the change of use takes place.

Once the initial notice has ceased to have effect, the approved inspector will be unable to give a final certificate and the local authority's powers to enforce the Building Regulations can revive. This has the consequences described in paragraph 2.30 below. A local authority can, however, extend the appropriate period of grace either before or after it expires, and may wish to if it is reasonably confident that a final certificate will be given soon.

Withdrawal of approved inspector

2.27 If an approved inspector for any reason cannot continue to supervise work for which he has given an initial notice he must inform you and the local authority by cancelling the initial notice. If you become aware that he is unable to continue supervising the work you must cancel the initial notice yourself. See s. 52 of the Building Act and Regulation 19 of the Approved Inspectors Regulations.

It is possible for the person carrying out the work to give a new initial notice jointly with a new approved inspector, provided that the new notice is accompanied by an undertaking by the original approved inspector that he will cancel the earlier notice as soon as the new notice is accepted (see paragraph 12 in schedule 3 to the Approved Inspectors Regulations).

Change of person intending to carry out work

2.28 Under section 51C of the Building Act, an approved inspector and a person who proposes to carry out work in succession to the person who gave the initial notice may jointly give a written notice to that effect to the local authority. The initial notice is then treated as having been given by the approved inspector and the new person intending to carry out the work.

Local authority's powers in relation to partially completed work

2.29 When an initial notice ceases to be in force and you do not engage another approved inspector, the local authority becomes responsible for enforcing the Regulations in relation to any work which has been carried out and for which a final certificate has not been given (see Regulation 20 of the Approved Inspectors Regulations).

In that event, you must provide the local authority on request with plans of the building work so far carried out. Additionally, if a plans certificate has been given for any part of the work you must supply the local authority with a copy of the plans referred to in the certificate.

You may be required by the local authority to cut into, lay open or pull down work so that it may ascertain whether any work not covered by a final certificate contravenes the Regulations. However, the local authority cannot take action against you in relation to any work described in a plans certificate which has been carried out in accordance with the plans to which the certificate relates.

If you intend to continue with partially completed work, you must give the local authority sufficient plans to show that the work can be completed without contravention of the Building Regulations. You must also pay the local authority the fee appropriate to that work.

Contravention of Building Regulations

2.30 Unlike a local authority an approved inspector has no power to enforce the Regulations. He may, however, inform you by written notice if he believes that any work being carried out under his supervision contravenes the Regulations. If you fail to remedy the alleged contravention within 3 months he is obliged to cancel the initial notice. He must give you and the local authority a cancellation notice in the prescribed form. This notice must specify the nature of the contravention unless a further initial notice relating to the work has been given and accepted. (See the Building Act, section 52 and Regulation 19 of the Approved Inspectors Regulations).

Dealing with variations to the work

2.31 Where it is proposed to vary work which is the subject of an initial notice (e.g. building six units instead of five on a site) you and your approved inspector should give an amendment notice to the local authority. (See the Building Act, section 51A and 51B and Regulation 9 of the Approved Inspectors Regulations).

Contents of an amendment notice

2.32 There is a prescribed form for an amendment notice (form 2 in Schedule 2 to the Approved Inspectors Regulations). It must contain the information which is required for an initial notice (see paragraph 2.18) plus either:

a)   a statement to the effect that all plans submitted with the original notice remain unchanged; or

b)   copies of all the amended plans with a statement that any plans not included remain unchanged.

Acceptance and rejection of amendment notice

2.33 The local authority has 5 working days in which to consider the notice and it may only reject it on prescribed grounds. The procedure is identical to that for acceptance or rejection of an initial notice (see paragraph 2.19).

Duration of validity of Initial Notices and Plans Certificates

2.34 Under section 52(5) of the Building Act, a local authority may cancel an initial notice if the work does not appear to have started within three years, beginning on the date that the notice was accepted or deemed to have been accepted. Under section 50(8), a local authority may likewise rescind its acceptance of a plans certificate after three years if the work does not appear to have begun.

UNAUTHORISED BUILDING WORK

Regularisation certificates

2.35 Carrying out work without notifying the local authority is a contravention of the Regulations. In relevant circumstances the local authority may take action under section 36 as outlined in paragraph 2.13. In the case of unauthorised work commenced on or after the

11th November 1985 the owner may apply to the local authority for a regularisation certificate. A fee, which is not refundable, must be paid when the application is made.

Regulation 21 lists the information to be given in an application for a regularisation certificate. This will include plans of the unauthorised work and plans showing any additional work needed to ensure compliance with the Regulations which were in force at the time the work was originally carried out.

On receipt of the application the local authority may require the owner to lay open the work or make tests and provide samples of materials in order that it can decide what work, if any, is needed to ensure compliance.

When satisfied that it has sufficient information the local authority will notify the owner of the work, if any, which is needed to comply with the relevant requirements of the Regulations, taking into account the results of any application for a dispensation or relaxation that may have been made. If this work is completed to its satisfaction the local authority can give a regularisation certificate to the owner.

THE TWO SYSTEMS OF BUILDING CONTROL

Summary Chart

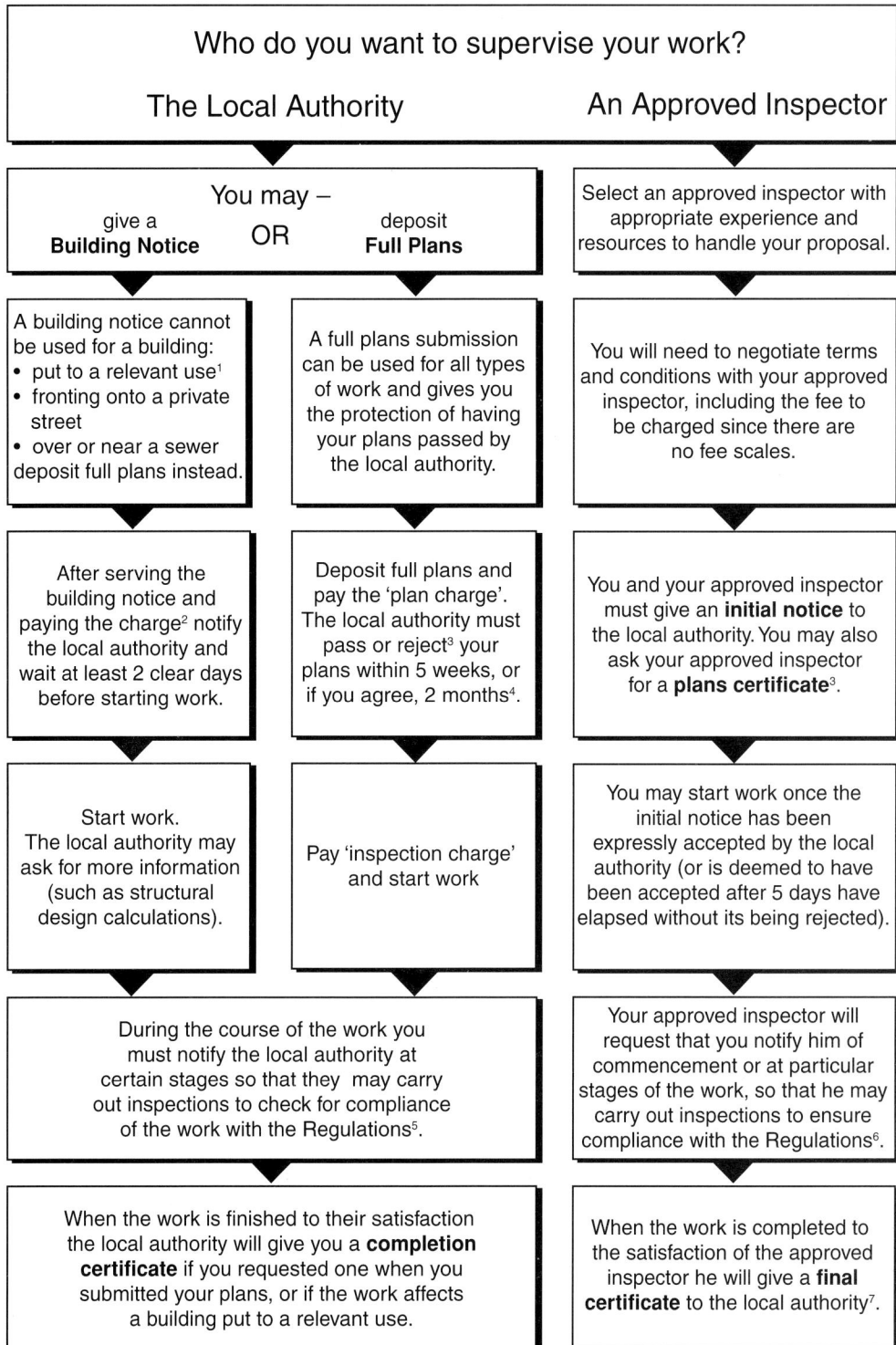

Who do you want to supervise your work?
The Local Authority   **An Approved Inspector**

The Local Authority

You may –
give a **Building Notice**   OR   deposit **Full Plans**

give a Building Notice	deposit Full Plans
A building notice cannot be used for a building: • put to a relevant use[1] • fronting onto a private street • over or near a sewer deposit full plans instead.	A full plans submission can be used for all types of work and gives you the protection of having your plans passed by the local authority.
After serving the building notice and paying the charge[2] notify the local authority and wait at least 2 clear days before starting work.	Deposit full plans and pay the 'plan charge'. The local authority must pass or reject[3] your plans within 5 weeks, or if you agree, 2 months[4].
Start work. The local authority may ask for more information (such as structural design calculations).	Pay 'inspection charge' and start work

During the course of the work you must notify the local authority at certain stages so that they may carry out inspections to check for compliance of the work with the Regulations[5].

When the work is finished to their satisfaction the local authority will give you a **completion certificate** if you requested one when you submitted your plans, or if the work affects a building put to a relevant use.

An Approved Inspector

Select an approved inspector with appropriate experience and resources to handle your proposal.

You will need to negotiate terms and conditions with your approved inspector, including the fee to be charged since there are no fee scales.

You and your approved inspector must give an **initial notice** to the local authority. You may also ask your approved inspector for a **plans certificate**[3].

You may start work once the initial notice has been expressly accepted by the local authority (or is deemed to have been accepted after 5 days have elapsed without its being rejected).

Your approved inspector will request that you notify him of commencement or at particular stages of the work, so that he may carry out inspections to ensure compliance with the Regulations[6].

When the work is completed to the satisfaction of the approved inspector he will give a **final certificate** to the local authority[7].

---

1 These include most places of work, hotels, boarding houses, offices, shops, railway premises and factories.

2 The charge payable is equivalent to the sum of the plan charge and the inspection charge and is payable in one instalment when the notice is given.

3 If the local authority reject your plans or the approved inspector is unable to give a plans certificate you may ask the Secretary of State for a determination and a fee is payable. See Section 3 of this Manual for full details.

4 You do not need to wait for the plans to be passed before starting work but if they are found to be defective you may have to alter some of the work you have already completed.

5 If the local authority considers that work contravenes the Regulations it may serve a notice requiring you to take it down or alter it. If you do not accept the views of the local authority there are ways of challenging it, see Section 3 of this Manual.

6 Your approved inspector may give you formal notice if he considers that the work contravenes the Regulations. If you have not remedied the contravention within 3 months of a written notice of contravention he must cancel the initial notice. The local authority may then take over responsibility, or you may engage another approved inspector if the local authority has taken no positive step to supervise the work. If you do not accept his view there are ways of challenging it, see Section 3 of this Manual.

7 The local authority has 10 days in which to reject the final certificate. Its acceptance prevents the local authority from giving a Section 36 notice (or prosecuting under Section 35) if it considers there is a contravention of the Regulations for your particular scheme.

Section 3

MEETING THE REQUIREMENTS OF THE BUILDING REGULATIONS

Contents

Flow Chart

```
                              ┌─────────────┐
                              │    START    │
                              └─────────────┘
                                     │
                                     ▼
┌──────────────────────┐      ◇─────────────────◇      ┌──────────────────────┐
│ You must follow one of│      │ Do The Building   │      │ Even if the Regulations│
│ the procedures described│◄YES│ Regulations       │ NO► │ do not apply to your   │
│ in Section 2¹ and the │      │ apply to your     │      │ proposal there may be  │
│ work must comply with │      │ proposal?         │      │ other legislation which│
│ the requirements of   │      │ - See Section 1.  │      │ does - See Section 4.  │
│ Schedule 1 to the     │      ◇─────────────────◇      └──────────────────────┘
│ Regulations.          │
└──────────────────────┘
```

Do The Building Regulations apply to your proposal? - See Section 1.

YES → You must follow one of the procedures described in Section 2[1] and the work must comply with the requirements of Schedule 1 to the Regulations.

NO → Even if the Regulations do not apply to your proposal there may be other legislation which does - See Section 4.

Does your proposal involve a material change of use? See Section1, paragraph 1.9.

YES → You must carry out any additional work needed to make the building, or the part being put to the new use, comply with the requirements of schedule 1 specified in Reg 6.

NO ↓

Turn to Schedule 1. Consider each requirement and its limits of application (if any). Does the requirement apply to your proposal?

NO → You need not satisfy that requirement, but other legislation may be relevant – see the explanatory notes opposite the text of Schedule 1 reproduced in Section 3.

YES ↓

Do you consider that any of the Schedule 1 requirements are too onerous or should not be applied to your proposal?

YES → You can apply to the local authority for a **relaxation** or **dispensation** of the requirement. If they refuse you can appeal. See Section 3, paragraphs 3.18 to 3.21.

NO →

The Approved Documents offer ready-made solutions which are likely to meet the requirements. Do you wish to use these?

YES → The relevant Approved Document is indicated in the explanatory notes opposite the text of Schedule 1 reproduced in Section 3.

NO → The local authority or approved inspector will have to be satisfied with your method of meeting the requirements.

Have the local authority or approved inspector said that your plans do not meet the Regulation requirements even though you believe that they do?

YES → You can apply to the Secretary of State for a **Determination**. See Section 3, paragraphs 3.14 to 3.17.

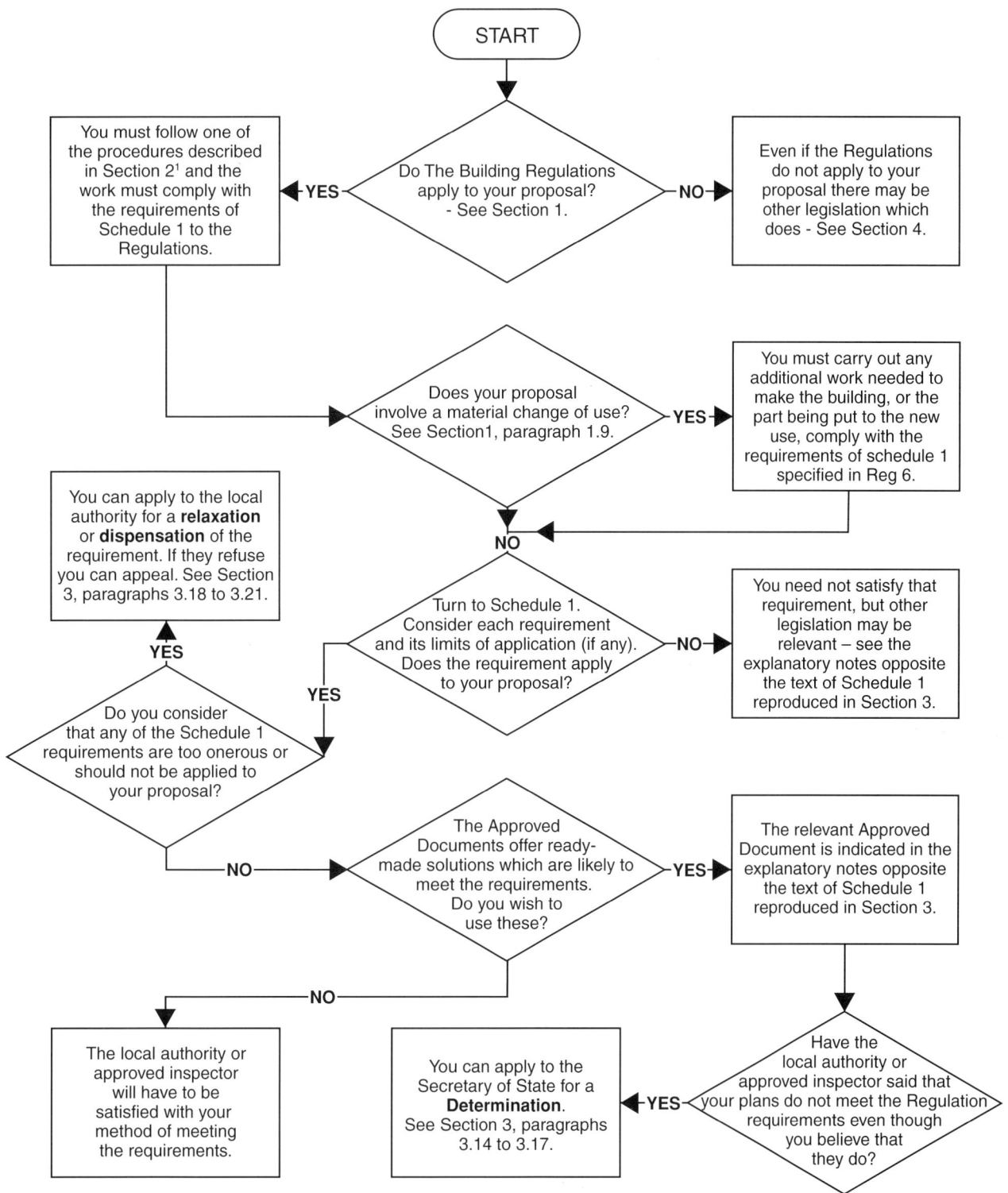

1 This is not necessary for the installation of a heat producing gas appliance by a person approved in accordance with the Gas Safety (Installation and Use) Regulations 1998 (see Regulation 12(5)).

Introduction

3.1 The Building Regulations 2000* are set out in full in this part of the manual together with some explanatory notes. The technical requirements are set out in Schedule 1 to the Regulations and the notes opposite the Schedule 1 requirements also refer to the relevant 'Approved Documents' as explained below.

Approved Documents

3.2 Approved Documents give general guidance as well as practical guidance about some of the ways of meeting the requirements of the Regulations. They are approved by the Secretary of State under the powers in section 6 of the Building Act. Approved Documents cover each of the parts of Schedule 1 to the Regulations and there is also an Approved Document which gives guidance on meeting Regulation 7. In addition, there are Approved Documents on two topics relating to dwellings. You will find a list of all the Approved Documents in Section 5.

Using the Approved Documents

3.3 The guidance in the Approved Documents does not constitute a set of statutory requirements and does not have to be followed if you wish to design and construct your building work in some other way which nevertheless can still be shown to comply with the applicable requirements of the Building Regulations. This guidance will be taken into account when a local authority or an approved inspector (as the building control body) is considering whether your plans of proposed work, or work in progress, complies with particular requirements. In addition, there is a legal presumption that following the guidance is evidence tending to support compliance with the Building Regulations. However, it is the building control body's duty to consider whether your plans comply with the functional requirements in the Building Regulations - not whether your plans necessarily accord with the general guidance or a specific example in an Approved Document.

3.4 If you choose not to follow the guidance you could, if necessary, be asked to demonstrate by other means that you have satisfied the requirements. You should bear in mind that in relation to Parts A to K and N (except for paragraphs H2 and J6), nothing needs to be done beyond what is necessary to secure reasonable standards of health and safety (Regulation 8). H 2 and J6 excluded as they contain requirements related to preventing the contamination of groundwater.

Parts L and M, are excluded as they deal, respectively, with conservation of fuel and power, and access and facilities for disabled people.

3.5 Approved Documents may give guidance in more than one form. They may describe particular methods of construction (Technical Solutions), give references to other publications (Alternative Approaches) or give acceptable levels of performance.

Technical solutions

3.6 Technical Solutions describe some of the more widely used forms of construction which achieve an acceptable level of performance. Although they generally give detailed guidance, in some cases they are written to give you sufficient flexibility to adapt them to suit a method of construction which you prefer.

Alternative approaches

3.7 If there is no Technical Solution that you wish to use or adapt, you should see if there is an alternative approach. This is usually based on the relevant recommendations of a named standard (see also paragraph 3.10) and may give you an opportunity to use a more complex procedure to 'fine tune' your solution.

Acceptable levels of performance

3.8 Some Approved Documents also contain an acceptable level of performance. This may be a useful guide if neither of the other two approaches is suitable for your proposals. The acceptable level should not be seen as a minimum standard, there may be circumstances where something less may satisfy the requirements of Schedule 1.

Materials and workmanship

3.9 An Approved Document in support of Regulation 7 – Materials and Workmanship – gives guidance on how you can show that you have complied with this requirement. You may show this in a number of ways including, for example:

- the appropriate use of a product bearing a CE marking in accordance with the Construction Products Directive[†];

- use of a material covered by a national or European certificate issued by European Technical Approvals issuing bodies, and the conditions of use are in accordance with the terms of the certificate;

- by complying with an appropriate technical specification. This could be a British Standard or another national

---

* The Building Regulations 2000 have been amended once since first publication. The version shown in this Manual consolidates this amendment as at October 2001.
† Construction Products Directive (89/106EEC) as amended by the CE marking Directive (93/68/EEC).

technical specification of any state which is a contracting party to the European Economic Area and which is equivalent, in use, to a British Standard, but see 3.11;

- past experience of the material or method of use showing that it is capable of performing its intended function;

- tests and calculations carried out in laboratories accredited and recognised by Member States of the EU, and recognised by the State's government.

National Standards and Technical Specifications

3.10 Some of the Approved Documents refer to specific National Standards (usually British Standards). In each case, the appropriate version of the Standard is listed at the back of the Approved Document. However, if this version has been revised, the new version may be used provided that it continues to address the relevant requirements of the Regulations. Many national standards are being replaced by European Standards. In the UK these are identified by the abbreviation BS EN XXXX.

3.11 National Standards sometimes cover aspects of performance which go beyond the requirements of the Regulations; for example, they may cover recommendations for good practice. The guidance in Standards and Technical Approvals is only relevant to compliance with the Regulations where it concerns health and safety (Parts A to K and N, but see the exception in paragraph 3.4), conservation of energy (Part L) or access and facilities for disabled people (Part M). In the absence of European Standards, European Technical Approvals will be made available, and these will replace conflicting national approvals.

Workplace (Health, Safety and Welfare) Regulations 1992

3.12 Generally, if you satisfy the requirements of the Building Regulations you will also satisfy any corresponding requirements of the Workplace Regulations.

MEETING THE REQUIREMENTS OF THE BUILDING REGULATIONS – RESOLVING QUESTIONS OF COMPLIANCE

Introduction

3.13 The local authority or approved inspector (as the building control body) must judge your plans/proposals against the applicable requirements in the Building Regulations, not the guidance in the Approved Documents. That guidance does not constitute a set of

statutory requirements and does not have to be followed if you wish to design and construct your building work in some other way which can still be shown to comply with the requirements of the regulations.

3.14 If, nevertheless, you are unable to reach agreement with the local authority or approved inspector about the compliance of your plans or building work with the Building Regulations, the Building Act 1984 contains two procedures - **determinations** and **appeals** - which provide for the Secretary of State for Transport, Local Government and the Regions or the National Assembly for Wales (NAW) (as appropriate) to adjudicate in such disputes. These procedures can apply either where:

(a) the local authority or approved inspector says that your plans for proposed building work do not comply with one or more of the requirements of the regulations, but you believe that they do; or

(b) you believe that one or more of the requirements of the regulations is/are too onerous or inappropriate in your particular circumstances and should either be relaxed or dispensed with, but the local authority has refused your application to do so under section 8 of the 1984 Act (approved inspectors do not have the power to consider such applications).

Determinations

3.15 In the case of the procedure in 3.14 (a) above, it may be appropriate for you to apply for a **determination** under either section 16(10)(a) or section 50(2) of the 1984 Act. Where a local authority is the building control body (section 16(10)(a)), once plans have been deposited for approval under the full plans procedure and a question arises during that procedure as to whether the plans of the proposed work conform with the Building Regulations, then that question can be referred by you to the Secretary of State/NAW for determination. However, the determination procedure is not available for building work being progressed by a building notice. Where an approved inspector is the building control body (section 50(2)), you can apply for a determination if the inspector refuses to give you a plans certificate on the grounds that he believes your plans do not conform with the Building Regulations. A fee is payable for a determination (i.e. half of the local authority's plan charge, excluding VAT, with a minimum fee of £50 and a maximum of £500).

Appeals

3.16 In the case of the procedure in 3.14 (b) above, you can **appeal** to the Secretary of State/NAW against the local authority's refusal to relax or dispense with the requirement(s) of the Building Regulations in question under section 39 of the 1984 Act. You must lodge the appeal within one month of receiving notification of the local authority's refusal but, unlike a determination, the appeal may relate to either plans of proposed building work or to work already under construction or completed. The appeal procedure can also be used whether you have used the full plans or building notice procedure to progress your work. No fee is payable for an appeal.

Guidance

3.17 The DTLR/NAW have jointly published 'A Guide to Determinations and Appeals' dated November 2001 which explains in more detail the purpose of, and the distinction between, determinations and appeals and how to proceed with an application/appeal. In particular, the guide explains why an application for a determination - which should be made before building work has substantially commenced - is likely to be the more appropriate procedure to resolve a disagreement about compliance with the Building Regulations. In this context the guide also explains that because the requirements in the Building Regulations have changed since 1985 and are now written in 'functional' – as opposed to 'prescriptive' – terms, it is likely to be very difficult to make a case for an application (and any subsequent appeal) to relax or dispense with a requirement unless very special circumstances exist.

3.18 Copies of the guide are available free of charge from DTLR Free Literature – see section 5 of this Manual. The guide can also be found on the DTLR website: www.safety.dtlr.gov.uk/bregs/app-det/app-det.htm.

Summary Chart

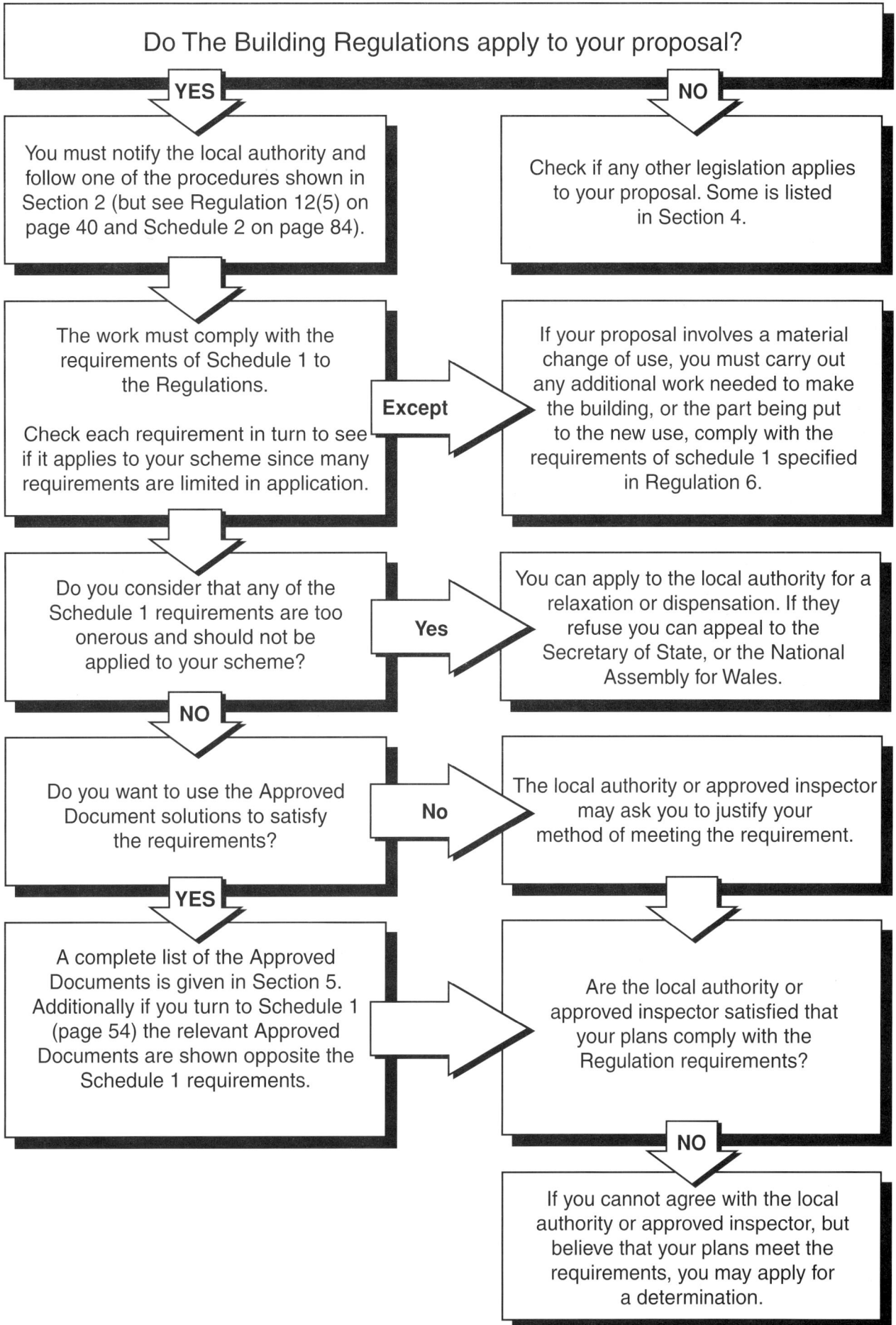

Do The Building Regulations apply to your proposal?

YES

You must notify the local authority and follow one of the procedures shown in Section 2 (but see Regulation 12(5) on page 40 and Schedule 2 on page 84).

NO

Check if any other legislation applies to your proposal. Some is listed in Section 4.

The work must comply with the requirements of Schedule 1 to the Regulations.

Check each requirement in turn to see if it applies to your scheme since many requirements are limited in application.

Except

If your proposal involves a material change of use, you must carry out any additional work needed to make the building, or the part being put to the new use, comply with the requirements of schedule 1 specified in Regulation 6.

Do you consider that any of the Schedule 1 requirements are too onerous and should not be applied to your scheme?

Yes

You can apply to the local authority for a relaxation or dispensation. If they refuse you can appeal to the Secretary of State, or the National Assembly for Wales.

NO

Do you want to use the Approved Document solutions to satisfy the requirements?

No

The local authority or approved inspector may ask you to justify your method of meeting the requirement.

YES

A complete list of the Approved Documents is given in Section 5. Additionally if you turn to Schedule 1 (page 54) the relevant Approved Documents are shown opposite the Schedule 1 requirements.

Are the local authority or approved inspector satisfied that your plans comply with the Regulation requirements?

NO

If you cannot agree with the local authority or approved inspector, but believe that your plans meet the requirements, you may apply for a determination.

The Building Regulations 2000 and Explanatory Notes

S.I. 2000 No. 2531

The Secretary of State, in exercise of the powers conferred upon him by sections 1(1), 3(1), 5, 8(2), 35 and 126 of, and paragraphs 1, 2, 4, 7 and 8, of Schedule 1 to, the Building Act 1984 and of all other powers enabling him in that behalf, after consulting the Building Regulations Advisory Committee and such other bodies as appear to him to be representative of the interests concerned in accordance with section 14(3) of that Act, hereby makes the following Regulations:-

PART I: GENERAL

Citation and commencement

1.- (1)   These Regulations may be cited as the Building Regulations 2000 and shall come into force on 1st January 2001.

Interpretation

2.- (1)   In these Regulations unless the context otherwise requires-

"the Act" means the Building Act 1984;

"amendment notice" means a notice given under section 51A of the Act;

"building" means any permanent or temporary building but not any other kind of structure or erection, and a reference to a building includes a reference to part of a building;

"building notice" means a notice given in accordance with regulations 12(2)(a) and 13;

"building work" has the meaning given in regulation 3(1);

"controlled service or fitting" means a service or fitting in relation to which Part G, H, J or L of Schedule 1 imposes a requirement;

"day" means any period of 24 hours commencing at midnight and excludes any Saturday, Sunday, Bank holiday or public holiday;

"dwelling" includes a dwelling-house and a flat;

"dwelling-house" does not include a flat or a building containing a flat;

"energy rating" of a dwelling means a numerical indication of the overall energy efficiency of that dwelling obtained by the application of a procedure approved by the Secretary of State under regulation 16(2) of these Regulations;

"European Technical Approval issuing body" means a body authorised by a member state of the European Economic Area to issue European Technical Approvals (a favourable technical assessment of the fitness for use of a construction product for the purposes of the Construction Products Directive;

"final certificate" means a certificate given under section 51 of the Act;

"flat" means separate and self-contained premises constructed or adapted for use for residential purposes and forming part of a building from some other part of which it is divided horizontally;

"floor area" means the aggregate area of every floor in a building or extension, calculated by reference to the finished internal faces of the walls enclosing the area, or if at any point there is no such wall, by reference to the outermost edge of the floor;

"fronting" has the meaning given in section 203(3) of the Highways Act 1980;

"full plans" means plans deposited with a local authority for the purposes of section 16 of the Act in accordance with regulations 12(2)(b) and 14;

"height" means the height of the building measured from the mean level of the ground adjoining the outside of the external walls of the building to the level of half the vertical height of the roof of the building, or to the top of the walls or of the parapet, if any, whichever is the higher;

EXPLANATORY NOTES

1 (1) The text of the Regulations which is reproduced here is an unofficial consolidation of the Building Regulations 2000 and the Building (Amendment) Regulations 2001, S.I.2001 No. 3335. The Building (Amendment) Regulations 2001 are subject to transitional provisions and none of them take effect before 1 April 2002. The SI amends regulations and requirements in connection with Parts H, J and L and make consequential amendments to the Building Act 1984. DTLR circular 03/2001 explains the transitional provisions in detail.

2 (1) Act - Building Act 1984, (1984 c. 55) as amended.

Building - This definition is narrower than the one contained in section 121 of the Building Act 1984. Its purpose is to restrict the scope of the Regulations to what are commonly thought of and referred to as buildings. The word building can mean part of a building. In the Department's view, a marquee is not a building.

Final certificate - this relates to the Approved Inspector system of building control (see Section 2 above)

Flat – This definition covers 'maisonettes' as well as flats.

Full plans – The word 'plans' is defined in section 126 of the Building Act 1984 as including drawings of any other description, and also specifications or other information in any form.

"initial notice" means a notice given under section 47 of the Act;

"institution" means an institution (whether described as a hospital, home, school or other similar establishment) which is used as living accommodation for, or for the treatment, care or maintenance of persons-

(a) suffering from disabilities due to illness or old age or other physical or mental incapacity, or

(b) under the age of five years, where such persons sleep on the premises;

"material alteration" has the meaning given in regulation 3(2);

"material change of use" has the meaning given in regulation 5;

"private street" has the meaning given in section 203(2) of the Highways Act 1980;

"public body's final certificate" means a certificate given under paragraph 3 of Schedule 4 to the Act;

"shop" includes premises-

(a) used for the sale to members of the public of food or drink for consumption on or off the premises,

(b) used for retail sales by auction to members of the public,

(c) used by members of the public as a barber or hairdresser, or for the hiring of any item, and

(d) where members of the public may take goods for repair or other treatment.

(2) In these Regulations "public building" means a building consisting of or containing-

(a) a theatre, public library, hall or other place of public resort;

(b) a school or other educational establishment not exempted from the operation of building regulations by virtue of section 4(1)(a) of the Act; or

(c) a place of public worship;

but a building is not to be treated as a place of public resort because it is, or it contains, a shop, storehouse or warehouse, or is a dwelling to which members of the public are occasionally admitted.

(3) Any reference in these Regulations to a numbered regulation, Part or Schedule is a reference to the regulation, Part or Schedule so numbered in these Regulations.

PART II: CONTROL OF BUILDING WORK

Meaning of building work

3.- (1) In these Regulations "building work" means--

(a) the erection or extension of a building;

(b) subject to paragraph (1A), the provision or extension of a controlled service or fitting in or in connection with a building;

(c) the material alteration of a building, or a controlled service or fitting, as mentioned in paragraph (2);

(d) work required by regulation 6 (requirements relating to a material change of use);

(e) the insertion of insulating material into the cavity wall of a building;

(f) work involving the underpinning of a building.

Initial notice - this relates to the Approved Inspector system of building control (see Section 2 above).

2 (2)(b) As a result of the repeal of Regulation 8 of the Education (Schools and Further and Higher Education) Regulations (SI 1989/351), schools in England are no longer exempt from the Building Regulations. See also paragraph 1.2 in Section 1 of this Manual. It is expected that schools in Wales will lose their exemption in early 2002.

3 (1)(b) Controlled services and fitting are those in relation to which Parts G, H, J and L impose requirements. They include sanitary equipment, heating and hot water systems, and drainage and waste disposal systems.

3 (1)(c) Not all alterations are subject to the Regulations, only those which are called material alterations' as defined in 3(2). Where a material alteration is carried out the Regulations apply to the building work regardless of when the building was constructed.

3 (1)(d) Regulation 6 may require work to be carried out in consequence of making a material change of use. Only certain classes of change of use are material for the purposes of the Regulations and these are defined in Regulation 5.

3 (1)(e) The insertion of insulation into an existing cavity wall is building work and is subject to control. The work must comply with C4 (resistance to weather and ground moisture) and D1 (cavity insulation) in Schedule 1. The building notice procedure provides for the local authority to be given certain information about the insulating material to be used and whether or not the installer is approved. (See Regulation 13(3)).

3 (1)(f) The underpinning of a building is considered to be building work in its own right.

(1A)   The provision or extension of a controlled service or fitting -

    (a)   in or in connection with an existing dwelling; and

    (b)   being a service or fitting in relation to which paragraph L1 , but not Part G, H or J, of Schedule 1 imposes a requirement, shall only be building work where that work consists of the provision of a window, rooflight, roof window, door (being a door which together with its frame has more than 50 per cent of its internal face area glazed), a space heating or hot water service boiler, or a hot water vessel.

(2)   An alteration is material for the purposes of these Regulations if the work, or any part of it, would at any stage result-

    (a)   in a building or controlled service or fitting not complying with a relevant requirement where previously it did; or

    (b)   in a building or controlled service or fitting which before the work commenced did not comply with a relevant requirement, being more unsatisfactory in relation to such a requirement.

(3)   In paragraph (2) "relevant requirement" means any of the following applicable requirements of Schedule 1, namely-

Part A (structure)

paragraph B1 (means of warning and escape)

paragraph B3 (internal fire spread-structure)

paragraph B4 (external fire spread)

paragraph B5 (access and facilities for the fire service)

Part M (access and facilities for disabled people)

Requirements relating to building work

4.-   (1)   Building work shall be carried out so that--

    (a)   it complies with the applicable requirements contained in Schedule 1; and

    (b)   in complying with any such requirement there is no failure to comply with any other such requirement.

(2)   Building work shall be carried out so that, after it has been completed-

    (a)   any building which is extended or to which a material alteration is made; or

    (b)   any building in, or in connection with, which a controlled service or fitting is provided, extended or materially altered; or

    (c)   any controlled service or fitting, complies with the applicable requirements of Schedule 1 or, where it did not comply with any such requirement, is no more unsatisfactory in relation to that requirement than before the work was carried out.

3 (1A) Where the work is to an existing building and consists of the provision of a window, rooflight, roof window, door (which together with its frame has more than 50 per cent of its internal face area glazed), a space heating or hot water service boiler, or a hot water vessel, it is building work, but otherwise the provision or extension in existing dwellings of controlled services and fittings is not building work if only Part L1 imposes requirements in relation to the services and fittings. Therefore the provision or extension in an existing dwelling of (e.g.) lighting systems in not building work.

3 (2) Alterations are only considered to be 'material' if they would affect the existing building as regards Part A, B1, B3, B4, B5 or Part M. This means that during the period of the works, and on completion, the alterations should not result in:

(a) a failure to comply with the Regulations where the existing building, service or fitting already complies; or

(b) a greater contravention of the Regulations where the existing building, service or fitting already fails to comply.

Therefore, where work is done to an existing building, service or fitting, the work itself must comply with all the current relevant requirements of Schedule 1, but the existing building must not be adversely affected. This means that while it will not usually be necessary to bring the building up to the standards of the Regulations, it should not be made worse as measured by the standards of the relevant requirements in Schedule 1.

Examples of material alterations are:

Removing part of a load-bearing wall which consequently requires the insertion of a beam to carry the load.

Altering a three-storey house in such a way that additional work is necessary to maintain the means of escape from the third storey.

Removing part of a wall which is non-loadbearing but is necessary for fire resistance.

It should be noted that building work involving a material alteration does not require access and facilities to be provided for disabled people if these are not already present in the existing building. However, where access and facilities are already provided it would be a contravention of the Regulations to take away or downgrade them (although it would be possible to re-site a disabled person's WC, for example).

4 (1) This regulation applies the applicable technical requirements of Schedule 1 to all building work (the applicable requirements are not limited to those listed in Regulation 3(3)).

Not all the requirements apply in all situations - the limitations are stated in the right hand column of Schedule 1. You must take care that in achieving compliance with one requirement you do not cause a contravention of another. For example, alteration work to an escape stair would be relevant building work because means of escape (B1) is a relevant requirement under Regulation 3(2). In carrying out the works, the requirements of K1 must be complied with or the stair made no less satisfactory if it did not already comply with K1.

Meaning of material change of use

5.-   For the purposes of paragraph 8(1)(e) of Schedule 1 to the Act and for the purposes of these Regulations, there is a material change of use where there is a change in the purposes for which or the circumstances in which a building is used, so that after that change-

(a)   the building is used as a dwelling, where previously it was not;

(b)   the building contains a flat, where previously it did not;

(c)   the building is used as an hotel or boarding house, where previously it was not;

(d)   the building is used as an institution, where previously it was not;

(e)   the building is used as a public building, where previously it was not;

(f)   the building is not a building described in Classes I to VI in Schedule 2, where previously it was; or

(g)   the building, which contains at least one dwelling, contains a greater or lesser number of dwellings than it did previously.

Requirements relating to material change of use

6.-   (1)   Where there is a material change of use of the whole of a building, such work, if any, shall be carried out as is necessary to ensure that the building complies with the applicable requirements of the following paragraphs of Schedule 1-

(a)   in all cases,   B1 (means of warning and escape)

    B2 (internal fire spread - linings)

    B3 (internal fire spread - structure)

    B4(2) (external fire spread - roofs)

    B5 (access and facilities for the fire service)

    F1 and F2 (ventilation)

    G1 (sanitary conveniences and washing facilities)

    G2 (bathrooms)

    H1 (foul water drainage)

    H6 (solid waste storage)

    J1 to J3 (combustion appliances)

    L1 (conservation of fuel and power -dwellings)

    L2 (conservation of fuel and power -buildings other than dwellings)

(b)   in the case of a material change of use described in regulations 5(c), (d), (e) or (f) A1 to A3 (structure);

(c)   in the case of a building exceeding fifteen metres in height, B4(1) (external fire spread - walls);

(d)   in the case of a material change of use described in regulation 5(a), C4 (resistance to weather and ground moisture); and,

(e)   in the case of a material change of use described in regulation 5(a), (b) or (g), E1 to E3 (resistance to the passage of sound).

  (2)   Where there is a material change of use of part only of a building, such work, if any, shall be carried out as is necessary to ensure that-

(a)   that part complies in all cases with any applicable requirement referred to in paragraph (1)(a);

(b)   in a case to which sub-paragraphs (b), (d) or (e) of paragraph (1) apply, that part complies with the requirements referred to in the relevant sub-paragraph; and

(c)   in a case to which sub-paragraph (c) of paragraph (1) applies, the whole building complies with the requirement referred to in that sub-paragraph.

5   Not every change of use of a building is subject to the Regulations. However, whilst, for example, a change from domestic use to office use is not subject to building regulations unless the change includes a material alteration, such a change of use may result in the premises being subject to the Fire Precautions Act 1971 and the Fire Precautions (Workplace) Regulations 1997 (as amended).

Regulation 5 defines the 'material changes of use' which are subject to the Building Regulations. Changes of use under planning legislation are a separate matter. If you are in doubt about the controls which apply to your proposal, you should consult the local authority department(s) concerned with building control and planning matters. Guidance on the application of Building Regulations to listed buildings is given in PPG 15, Planning Policy Guidance: Planning and the historic environment, PPG 15 September 1994, published by DETR, ISBN 0-11-752944-3.

6   (1)   On a material change of use of the whole if a building it is always necessary to ensure compliance with the relevant requirements listed in regulation 6(1)(a). In the particular cases referred to in 6(1)(b), (c), (d) and (e) these additional requirements must also be met. This may require building work to be done. It should be noted that sufficient work must be carried out to ensure that the entire building meets the specified requirements, not just any parts of the building that you intended to alter.

The need for compliance with requirement H1 (foul water drainage) was added by the Building (Amendment) Regulations 2001 (SI 2001 No. 3335)

6   (2)   Where there is a change of use to part only of a building, the general rule is that the requirements of regulation 6(1) only apply to that part of the building of which the use is to be changed, but where the building is more than 15m high the whole of the external walls must comply with requirement B4(1) of Schedule 1 - external fire spread - walls.

Materials and workmanship

7.- Building work shall be carried out-

   (a)   with adequate and proper materials which-

      (i)   are appropriate for the circumstances in which they are used,

      (ii) are adequately mixed and prepared, and

      (iii) are applied, used or fixed so as adequately to perform the functions for which they are designed; and

   (b)   in a workmanlike manner.

Limitation on requirements

8.   Parts A to K and N (except for paragraphs H2 and J6) of Schedule 1 shall not require anything to be done except for the purpose of securing reasonable standards of health and safety for persons in or about buildings (and any others who may be affected by buildings, or matters connected with buildings).

Exempt buildings and work

9.   These Regulations do not apply to-

   (a)   the erection of any building or extension of a kind described in Schedule 2; or

   (b)   the carrying out of any work to or in connection with such a building or extension, if after the carrying out of that work it is still a building or extension of a kind described in that Schedule.

PART III: EXEMPTION OF PUBLIC BODIES FROM PROCEDURAL REQUIREMENTS

The Metropolitan Police Authority

10.- (1)   The Metropolitan Police Authority is hereby prescribed for the purposes of section 5 of the Act (exemption of public bodies from the procedural requirements and enforcement of building regulations).

   (2)   The Metropolitan Police Authority is exempt from compliance with these Regulations in so far as the requirements in these Regulations are not substantive requirements.

PART IV: RELAXATION OF REQUIREMENTS

Power to dispense with or relax requirements

11.- (1)   The powers under section 8(1) of the Act to dispense with or relax any requirement contained in these Regulations shall be exercisable by the local authority.

   (2)   Any notification by the local authority to an applicant that they have refused his application to dispense with or relax any requirement of these Regulations shall inform the applicant of the effect of section 39(1) and (3) of the Act (appeal against refusal etc. to relax building regulations).

PART V: NOTICES AND PLANS

Giving of a building notice or deposit of plans

12.- (1)   In this regulation 'relevant use' means a use as a workplace of a kind to which Part II of the Fire Precautions (Workplace) Regulations 1997 applies or a use designated under section 1 of the Fire Precautions Act 1971.

7   (1)   Building work should be carried out with adequate and proper materials and in a workmanlike manner. These terms are explained in the Approved Document to support Regulation 7. The current edition of Regulation 7 and its Approved Document took effect on the 1 April 1999. The guidance on control of house longhorn beetle was removed from the Approved Document at that stage and will be incorporated into the next edition of Approved Document A which is currently under review. In the interim, the advice in the 1992 edition of the Approved Document to support Regulation 7 should still be considered applicable.

8   Under Section 1 of the Building Act, building regulations may be made for the main purpose of securing the health, safety, welfare and convenience of people in or about buildings, furthering the conservation of fuel and power and preventing waste, undue consumption, misuse or contamination of water. Regulation 8 limits the requirements of Parts A to K and N (except for paragraphs H2 and J6) of Schedule 1 to reasonable health and safety considerations only. Higher standards may be thought desirable for reasons of consumer satisfaction, but they are not necessary to satisfy these Parts. Parts L and M are concerned with conservation of fuel and power, and with access and facilities for disabled people.

9   Schedule 2 to the Regulations allows the erection of buildings which are to be put to certain specialised uses, temporary buildings and some small buildings and extensions to be exempt from control. Additionally, work carried out to such buildings is also exempt provided that after the work is completed it is still a building or extension of a kind described in that Schedule.

10   By virtue of the The Building Regulations (Amendment) Regulations 2000 (SI 2000 No. 1554) the Metropolitan Police Authority has been exempted from having to comply with the procedural requirements of building control, although it is still required to comply with the substantive or technical requirements of the Regulations. As an exempt body the Metropolitan Police Authority is also exempt from the enforcement procedures by local authorities.

11   All applications for a relaxation or dispensation of a requirement of the Regulations should be made to the local authority. Where the local authority refuse an application the applicant may appeal to the Secretary of State for Transport, Local Government and the Regions or if appropriate, the National Assembly for Wales, within one month of the date on which the local authority notify the refusal. If the local authority does not notify the applicant of its decision within 2 months (or such longer period as has been agreed) the applicant may appeal to the Secretary of State or the National Assembly as if it had refused. For further comments on relaxations and dispensations see paragraphs 3.18 to 3.21 of Section 3.

(2)   Subject to the following provisions of this regulation, a person who intends to carry out building work or to make a material change of use shall-

    (a)   give to the local authority a building notice in accordance with regulation 13; or

    (b)   deposit full plans with the local authority in accordance with regulation 14.

(3)   A person shall deposit full plans where he intends to carry out building work in relation to a building put or intended to be put to a use which is a relevant use.

(4)   A person shall deposit full plans where he intends to carry out work which includes the erection of a building fronting on to a private street.

(4A)   A person shall deposit full plans where he intends to carry out building work in relation to which paragraph H4 of Schedule 1 imposes a requirement.

(5)   A person who intends to carry out building work consisting only of the installation of a heat producing gas appliance is not required to give a building notice or deposit full plans if the appliance is to be installed by a person, or an employee of a person, approved in accordance with regulation 3 of the Gas Safety (Installation and Use) Regulations 1998.

(6)   Where regulation 20 of the Building (Approved Inspectors etc.) Regulations 2000 (local authority powers in relation to partly completed work) applies, the owner shall comply with the requirements of that regulation instead of with this regulation.

Particulars and plans where a building notice is given

13.- (1)   A building notice shall state the name and address of the person intending to carry out the work and shall be signed by him or on his behalf, and shall contain or be accompanied by-

    (a)   a statement that is given for the purposes of regulation 12(2)(a);

    (b)   a description of the proposed building work or material change of use; and

    (c)   particulars of the location of the building to which the proposal relates and the use or intended use of that building.

(2)   In the case of the erection or extension of a building, a building notice shall be accompanied by-

    (a)   a plan to a scale of not less than 1:1250 showing-

        (i)   the size and position of the building, or the building as extended, and its relationship to adjoining boundaries;

        (ii)   the boundaries of the curtilage of the building, or the building as extended, and the size, position and use of every other building or proposed building within that curtilage;

        (iii)   the width and position of any street on or within the boundaries of the curtilage of the building or the building as extended;

    (b)   a statement specifying the number of storeys (each basement level being counted as one storey), in the building to which the proposal relates; and

EXPLANATORY NOTES

12 (2)   A person intending to carry out building work who chooses to have it supervised by the local authority rather than by an approved inspector has the option of giving a building notice or depositing full plans. There are cases where the building notice option is not available – see Regulations 12(3), (4) and 4(A).

12 (3)   The option of giving a building notice is not available where a building is to be put to a use subject to the Fire Precautions Act 1971, or will be a workplace subject to the Fire Precautions (Workplace) Regulations 1997 (i.e. a 'relevant use'). Full plans must be deposited so that the local authority can carry out its obligation of consulting the fire authority under section 16 of the Fire Precautions Act 1971.

12 (4)   The option of giving a building notice is not available where a person intends to erect a building fronting onto a private street. The purpose of regulation 12(4) is to ensure that the operation of the advanced payments code of the Highways Act 1980 (ss 219 - 225) takes place. This requires that arrangements are made to meet the cost of providing street works before buildings are constructed in private streets.

12 (4A)   The option of giving a building notice is not available where a person intends to erect a building over a sewer. This is to allow consultation to take place with the sewerage undertaker under the provisions of regulation 14A. See Section 2, paragraph 2.5 above.

12 (5)   A person who intends only to install a heat-producing gas appliance need not inform the local authority provided that it is to be installed by a person (or an employee of a person) approved under the Gas Safety (Installation and use) Regulations 1998, SI 1998 No.2451 The Council for Registered Gas Installers (CORGI) has developed a certification scheme which requires that individual gas fitting operatives are assessed on their competence to carry out safe gas work. Details of the CORGI scheme are given in the Nationally Accredited Certification Scheme for individual gas fitting operatives. For current information contact: The Operations Support Department, CORGI, 1 Elmwood, Chineham Business Park, Crockford Lane, Basingstoke, Hampshire, RG24 9WG.

12 (6)   Where work has been carried out under the supervision of an Approved Inspector who withdraws before the work is complete the special requirements of Regulation 20 of the Building (Approved Inspectors etc) Regulations apply. They enable the local authority to require plans of the work (including plans of work for which a plans certificate has been given, but excluding any for which a final certificate has been given) and to require uncertified work to be uncovered. (See also paragraph 2.28 in Section 2).

13   Regulation 13 lists the information to be given in or with a building notice. For further comments on the use of the building notice procedure see paragraphs 2.8 and 2.9 in Section 2.

    (c)   particulars of-

        (i)   the provision to be made for the drainage of the building or extension;

        (ii)

        (iii) the steps to be taken to comply with any local enactment which applies.

(3)   In the case of building work which involves the insertion of insulating material into the cavity walls of a building, a building notice shall be accompanied by a statement which specifies-

    (a)   the name and type of insulating material to be used;

    (b)   the name of any European Technical Approval issuing body which has approved the insulating material;

    (c)   the requirements of Schedule 1 in relation to which any body referred to in (b) has approved the insulating material;

    (d)   any national standard of a member state of the European Economic Area to which the insulating material conforms; and

    (e)   the name of any body which has issued any current approval to the installer of the insulating material.

(4)   Where building work involves the provision of a hot water storage system in relation to which paragraph G3 in Schedule 1 (hot water storage) imposes a requirement, a building notice shall be accompanied by a statement which specifies-

    (a)   the name, make, model and type of hot water storage system to be installed;

    (b)   the name of the body, if any, which has approved or certified that the system is capable of performing in a way which satisfies the requirements of paragraph G3 of Schedule 1;

    (c)   the name of the body, if any, which has issued any current registered operative identity card to the installer or the proposed installer of the system.

(5)   Where a building notice has been given, a person carrying out building work or making a material change of use shall give the local authority, within such time as they specify, such plans as are, in the particular case, necessary for the discharge of their functions in relation to building regulations and are specified by them in writing.

(6)   Neither a building notice nor plans which accompany it or are given under paragraph (5) are to be treated for the purposes of section 16 of the Act as having been deposited in accordance with building regulations.

(7)   A building notice shall cease to have effect on the expiry of three years from the date on which that notice was given to the local authority, unless before the expiry of that period-

    (a)   the building work to which the notice relates was commenced; or

    (b)   the material change of use described in the notice was made.

Paragraph13(2)(c)(ii) relating to precautions to be taken when building over a sewer under s 18 of the Building Act 1984 was removed by the Building (Amendment) Regulations 2001 (SI 2001/3335), which inserted on equivalent paragraph into Regulation 14(3).

There may be a need to comply with local legislation in some areas. (See Section 4 Other Legislation)

13 (3) Where it is intended to insert insulating material into the cavity walls of an existing building the information listed in this sub-paragraph must be provided. Section 4 of Approved Document C gives advice on the circumstances and conditions in which such work can be satisfactorily carried out and recommends that it should be done by an approved installer. See also Approved Document D - Toxic substances (which covers measures to prevent permeation of toxic fumes from the insulant into the building).

13 (4) Where it is intended to install an unvented hot water system the information listed in this sub-paragraph must be provided. The Approved Document for requirement G3 recommends that work should be done by a competent person or an approved installer. Further information is given in the leaflet: Unvented hot water storage; available from: DLTR free literature, PO Box 236, Wetherby, West Yorkshire, LS23 7NB.

13 (5) Where the building notice procedure is used the local authority may nevertheless ask for such additional plans as are necessary in any particular case. 'Plans' includes drawings, specifications or other information in any form, and a local authority might well need information on matters which cannot be checked by inspection on site, such as structural calculations or specifications of materials used.

13 (6) The local authority has no function of passing or rejecting plans accompanying a building notice or any additional information which is provided under paragraph (5). Compliance with the requirements of the Regulations is ensured primarily by site inspections.

Full plans

14.- (1) Full plans shall be accompanied by a statement that they are deposited for the purpose of regulation 12(2)(b).

(2) (a) Full plans shall be deposited in duplicate, of which the local authority may retain one copy; and

(b) where Part B of Schedule 1 (Fire safety) imposes a requirement in relation to proposed building work, an additional two copies of any such plans as demonstrate compliance with that requirement shall be deposited, both of which may be retained by the local authority.

(3) Full plans shall consist of-

(a) a description of the proposed building work or material change of use, and the plans, particulars and statements required by paragraphs (1) to (4) of regulation 13; and

(aa) where paragraph H4 of Schedule 1 imposes a requirement, particulars of the precautions to be taken in building over a drain, sewer or disposal main to comply with the requirements of that paragraph; and

(b) any other plans which are necessary to show that the work would comply with these Regulations.

(4) Full plans shall be accompanied by a statement as to whether the building is put or is intended to be put to a use which is a relevant use as defined by regulation 12(1)

(5) Full plans may be accompanied by a request from the person carrying out building work that on completion of the work he wishes the local authority to issue a completion certificate in accordance with regulation 17.

(6) Paragraph (2)(b) shall not require the deposit of additional copies of plans where the proposed building work relates to the erection, extension or material alteration of a dwelling-house or flat.

Consultation with sewerage undertaker

14A.-(1) This regulation applies where full plans have been deposited with the local authority and paragraph H4 of Schedule 1 imposes requirements in relation to the building work which is the subject of those plans.

(2) Where this regulation applies the local authority shall consult the sewerage undertaker -

(a) as soon as practicable after the plans have been deposited; and

(b) before issuing any completion certificate in relation to the building work in accordance with regulation 17 pursuant to a request under regulation 14(5).

(3) Where a local authority is required by paragraph (2) to consult the sewerage undertaker they shall -

(a) give to the sewerage undertaker, in a case where they are consulting them following the deposit of full plans, sufficient plans to show whether the work would, if carried out in accordance with those plans, comply with the applicable requirements of paragraph H4 of Schedule 1;

(b) have regard to any views expressed by the sewerage undertaker; and

(c) not pass plans or issue a completion certificate until 15 days have elapsed from the date on which they consulted the sewerage undertaker, unless the sewerage undertaker has expressed its views to them before the expiry of that period.

14   In the case of the erection of a new building 'full plans' would be complete plans (ie plans of the whole building, the site etc.) In the case of work to an existing building 'full plans' would be those relevant to the proposed work. Since the reason for depositing full plans will normally be to have them passed, a person in doubt would be prudent to provide more information rather than less, to avoid the possibility of the plans being rejected on the grounds that they are defective by being incomplete.

14 (2)   Normally, two copies of the plans will need to be deposited with the local authority - one of which it will retain for its records. However, if the proposal needs to comply with Part B (Fire safety) a further two copies of the plans must be deposited so that the local authority can consult the fire authority (although this requirement for extra copies does not apply to building work to dwelling-houses and flats).

14 (3)   Full plans must contain all the information that would be included in a building notice and whatever other plans are necessary to show that the work will comply with the regulations.

See also Section 2 paragraph 2.5 above.

14 (4)   The local authority must be informed if the building is to be put to a designated use under the Fire Precautions Act (ie applies to hotels, boarding houses, offices, shops, railway premises and factories.) or will be used as a workplace of a kind to which Part II of the Fire Precautions (Workplace) Regulations 1997 applies.

14 (5)   The local authority will give a completion certificate (see Regulation 17) when the work is finished if requested to do so when the full plans submission is made, and if it is satisfied that the applicable requirements of Schedule 1 have been complied with.

For more information on the effect of passing of plans, and the procedures for stage and conditional approval see paragraphs 2.4 to 2.11 in Section 2.

14A   This regulation applies when it is proposed to build over or near an existing drain, sewer or disposal main shown on the sewerage undertaker's sewer records whether or not that sewer is a public sewer. Section 199 of the Water Industry Act 1991 places a duty on sewerage undertakers to keep records of public sewers and certain other pipes. The records must be kept separately for each local authority area and must be supplied free of charge to local authorities who must ensure that they are available for inspection by the public free of charge. The records must be presented in the form of a map.
The local authority is obliged to consult the sewerage undertaker as soon as practicable after plans have been deposited. It must supply to the sewerage undertaker sufficient plans to show that the work will comply with requirement H4 of Schedule 1 and must take into account any views expressed by the sewerage undertaker.
The plans must not be passed or a completion certificate issued until 15 days have elapsed from the date of the consultation unless the sewerage undertaker has expressed its views before that period of time has expired.

Notice of commencement and completion of certain stages of work

15.- (1) A person who proposes to carry out building work shall not commence that work unless-

(a) he has given the local authority notice that he intends to commence work; and

(b) at least two days have elapsed since the end of the day on which he gave the notice.

(2) A person carrying out building work shall not-

(a) cover up any excavation for a foundation, any foundation, any damp-proof course or any concrete or other material laid over a site; or

(b) cover up in any way any drain or sewer to which these Regulations apply, unless he has given the local authority notice that he intends to commence that work, and at least one day has elapsed since the end of the day on which he gave the notice.

(3) A person who has laid, haunched or covered any drain or sewer in respect of which Part H of Schedule 1 (drainage and waste disposal) imposes a requirement shall give notice to that effect to the local authority not more than five days after the completion of the work.

(4) A person carrying out building work shall, not more than five days after that work has been completed, give the local authority notice to that effect.

(5) Where a building is being erected, and that building (or any part of it) is to be occupied before completion, the person carrying out the work shall give the local authority at least five days notice before the building or any part of it is occupied.

(6) Where a person fails to comply with paragraphs (1) to (3), he shall comply within a reasonable time with any notice given by the local authority requiring him to cut into, lay open or pull down so much of the work as prevents them from ascertaining whether these Regulations have been complied with.

(7) If the local authority have given notice specifying the manner in which any work contravenes the requirements in these Regulations, a person who has carried out any further work to secure compliance with these Regulations shall within a reasonable time after the completion of such further work give notice to the local authority of its completion.

Energy rating

16.- (1) This regulation applies where a new dwelling is created by building work or by a material change of use in connection with which building work is carried out.

(2) Where this regulation applies, the person carrying out the building work shall calculate the energy rating of the dwelling by means of a procedure approved by the Secretary of State, and shall give notice of that rating to the local authority.

(3) The notice referred to in paragraph (2) shall be given not later than the date on which the notice required by paragraph (4) of regulation 15 is given, and, where a new dwelling is created by the erection of a building, it shall be given at least five days before occupation of the dwelling.

(4) Where this regulation applies, subject to paragraphs (6) and (7), the person carrying out the building work shall affix, as soon as practicable, in a conspicuous place in the dwelling, a notice stating the energy rating of the dwelling.

15   Regulation 15 requires the local authority to be notified before certain stages of work are carried out. Work may be commenced at any time after a building notice has been given, provided that the local authority is given at least 2 clear days notice. For full plans submissions See Section 2, paragraph 2.12.

If work is carried out without notification to the local authority at the stages specified in this regulation it may ask for the work to be taken down as far as is necessary for the local authority to check whether it complies with the Regulations. If the local authority then requires the work to be altered to secure compliance, it must be informed in writing when this is done.

This regulation does not apply if the work is to be supervised by an approved inspector.

16   When a dwelling is created (by building work or a material change of use) its energy rating must be calculated by the standard assessment procedure (SAP). This is explained and defined, along with appropriate reference data and a calculation worksheet, in "the Government's Standard Assessment Procedure for Energy Rating of Dwellings". The edition of the SAP currently approved for the purposes of Regulation 16 is the 1998 Edition. This is available from BRESCU Publications free of charge, tel: 01923 664258. A revised edition of the SAP is in preparation. It will be approved for the purposes of Regulation 16, in due course.

16 (3)   Notice of the energy rating must be given to the local authority or approved inspector not more than 5 days after the work has been completed. If the dwelling is occupied before completion, notice of the energy rating must be given to the local authority, not less than 5 days before occupation. There are equivalent provisions in Regulation 12 of the Approved Inspector Regulations, which apply in cases where work is supervised by an Approved Inspector. It should be noted that different time periods apply where the building is occupied before completion or where a dwelling is created by a material change of use (see Section 2 paragraph 2.25).

16 (4)   A notice which states the calculated energy rating of the dwelling must be fixed in a conspicuous place in the dwelling. In DETR Circular 07/2000 the Department suggested that the notice should be typed on A4 paper and placed in a suitable plastic holder for protection. It should be double-sided and should be attached by non-marking adhesive to a window near, or in, the front door. In flats (where there is no suitable window in or near the front door) it could be fixed to a sitting room or kitchen window.

(5)   The notice referred to in paragraph (4) shall be affixed not later than the date on which the notice required by paragraph (4) of regulation 15 is given, and, where a new dwelling is created by the erection of a building, it shall be affixed not later than five days before occupation of the dwelling.

(6)   Subject to paragraph (7), if, on the date the dwelling is first occupied as a residence, no notice has been affixed in the dwelling in accordance with paragraph (4), the person carrying out the building work shall, not later than the date on which the notice required by paragraph (4) of regulation 15 is given, give to the occupier of the dwelling a notice stating the energy rating of the dwelling calculated in accordance with paragraph (2).

(7)   Paragraphs (4) and (6) shall not apply in a case where the person carrying out the work intends to occupy, or occupies, the dwelling as a residence.

Completion certificates

17.- (1)   A local authority shall give a completion certificate in accordance with this regulation and as provided for in paragraph (2) where-

(a)   they receive a notice under regulation 15(4) or (5) that building work has been completed, or, that a building has been partly occupied before completion; and

(b)   they have either-

(i)   been notified in accordance with regulation 14(4) that the building is put or is intended to be put to a use which is a relevant use as defined by regulation 12(1); or

(ii)   been requested in accordance with regulation 14(5), to give a completion certificate.

(2)   Where in relation to any building work or, as the case may be, to any part of a building which has been occupied before completion, a local authority have been able to ascertain, after taking all reasonable steps in that behalf, that the relevant requirements of Schedule 1 specified in the certificate have been satisfied, they shall give a certificate to that effect.

(3)   In this regulation the relevant requirements mean-

(a)   in a case mentioned in paragraph (1)(b)(i), the applicable requirements of Part B of Schedule 1 (fire safety); and

(b)   in a case mentioned in paragraph (1)(b)(ii), any applicable requirements of Schedule 1.

(4)   A certificate given in accordance with this regulation shall be evidence (but not conclusive evidence) that the requirements specified in the certificate have been complied with.

PART VI: MISCELLANEOUS

Testing of building work

18.   The local authority may make such tests of any building work as may be necessary to establish whether it complies with regulation 7 or any of the applicable requirements contained in Schedule 1.

Sampling of material

19.   The local authority may take such samples of the material to be used in the carrying out of building work as may be necessary to enable them to ascertain whether such materials comply with the provisions of these Regulations.

EXPLANATORY NOTES

16 (5) The time periods for fixing the notice are identical to those referred to in the note to 16(3) above.

17 The local authority must be notified when building work has been completed or when a new building is to be occupied (see Regulation 15). On receipt of this notice, if it is satisfied that the relevant requirements of the Regulations have been met, it must issue a completion certificate to that effect if 17(1)(b) applies.

A completion certificate in respect of fire safety requirements must be issued where the building is to be put to a relevant use. A completion certificate in respect of all applicable requirements of Schedule 1 must be given if the local authority was requested to provide one when the full plans submission was made.

18 The local authority is permitted to test any building work to establish the extent of its compliance with regulation 7, or the applicable requirements of Schedule 1. For example, this permits the testing of drains and the carrying out of airtightness tests under the provisions of Part L . This regulation does not apply if the work is being supervised by an Approved Inspector

19 The local authority is permitted to take samples of the materials being used in the work to ensure that the materials comply with the requirements of the Regulations. See also Regulation 7 and its supporting Approved Document.

This regulation does not apply if the work is being supervised by an Approved Inspector, but similar provisions for testing now exist in the Approved Inspector regulations.

Supervision of building work otherwise than by local authorities

20.- (1) Regulations 12, 15, 16, 17, 18 and 19 shall not apply in respect of any work specified in an initial notice, an amendment notice or a public body's notice, which is in force.

(2) Regulations 18 and 19 shall not apply in respect of any work in relation to which a final certificate or a public body's final certificate has been accepted by the local authority.

Unauthorised building work

21.- (1) This regulation applies where it appears to a local authority that unauthorised building work has been carried out on or after 11th November 1985.

(2) In this regulation, 'unauthorised building work' means building work other than work in relation to which an initial notice, an amendment notice or a public body's notice has effect, which is done without-

(a) a building notice being given to the local authority; or

(b) full plans of the work being deposited with the local authority; or

(c) a notice of commencement of work being given, in accordance with regulation 15(1) of these Regulations, where a building notice has been given or full plans have been deposited.

(3) Where this regulation applies, the owner (in this regulation referred to as "the applicant") may apply in writing to the local authority for a regularisation certificate in accordance with this regulation, and shall send with his application-

(a) a statement that the application is made in accordance with this regulation,

(b) a description of the unauthorised work,

(c) so far as is reasonably practicable, a plan of the unauthorised work, and

(d) so far as is reasonably practicable, a plan showing any additional work required to be carried out to secure that the unauthorised work complies with the requirements relating to building work in the building regulations which were applicable to that work when it was carried out (in this regulation referred to as the relevant requirements).

(4) Where a local authority receive an application in accordance with this regulation, they may require the applicant to take such reasonable steps, including laying open the unauthorised work for inspection by the authority, making tests and taking samples, as the authority think appropriate to ascertain what work, if any, is required to secure that the relevant requirements are met.

(5) When the applicant has taken any such steps required by the local authority as are described in paragraph (4), and having had regard to any direction given in accordance with sections 8 and 9 of, and Schedule 2 to, the Act dispensing with or relaxing a requirement in building regulations which applies to the unauthorised work, the local authority shall notify the applicant-

(a) of the work which in their opinion is required to comply with the relevant requirements or those requirements as dispensed with or relaxed, or

(b) that they cannot determine what work is required to comply with the relevant requirements or those requirements as dispensed with or relaxed, or

(c) that no work is required to secure compliance with the relevant requirements or those requirements as dispensed with or relaxed.

(6) Where the local authority have been able to satisfy themselves, after taking all reasonable steps for that purpose that-

(a) the relevant requirements have been satisfied (taking account of any work carried out and any dispensation or relaxation given in accordance with sections 8 and 9 of, and Schedule 2 to, the Act), or

20   Where work is being carried out by an approved inspector (or work is being carried out by a public body approved in accordance with section 54 of the Building Act) the local authority has no responsibility for checking compliance with the requirements of Schedule 1 of the Regulations. Consequently Regulations 12, 15, 16, 17, 18 and 19 do not apply. Where such work has been completed and certified, Regulations 18 and 19 (the local authority's power to test building work and sample materials) remain dis-applied.

21   This regulation allows the owner of a building on which "authorised work" has been carried out since November 1985 to apply to the local authority for a "Regularisation Certificate". "Unauthorised work" is defined in Regulation 21(2). It is work done without observance of the procedural provisions calling for notification of building work to the local authority.

21 (3) Regulation 21(3) lists the information to be given in an application for a regularisation certificate. This will include plans of the unauthorised building work and plans showing any additional work which is needed to ensure that the unauthorised building work complies with the Regulations. (Note:- the work will need to comply with the Regulations which were in force at the time that the unauthorised work was carried out, therefore this date may need to be proved to the local authority.)

21 (4) When the local authority receives an application for a regularisation certificate it may require the owner to lay open the work or make tests and provide samples of materials in order that it can decide what work, if any, is needed to ensure compliance with the Regulations.

21 (5) When the local authority is satisfied that it has sufficient information it will notify the owner of any work that is needed (if any) in order to satisfy the relevant requirements of the Regulations. If a relaxation or dispensation of the Regulations (see paragraphs 3.18 to 3.21 in Section 3) has been approved the local authority must take this into account when assessing any work which is needed.

21 (6) If the local authority is satisfied that the work complies with the Regulations (i.e. those that were in force when the original unauthorised work was carried out) it may give the owner a regularisation certificate.

(b) no work is required to secure that the unauthorised work satisfies the relevant requirements (taking account of any such dispensation or relaxation), they may give a certificate to that effect (in this regulation referred to as "a regularisation certificate").

(7) A regularisation certificate shall be evidence (but not conclusive evidence) that the relevant requirements specified in the certificate have been complied with.

(8) Where this regulation applies, regulations 12 and 14 shall not apply, and neither the supply of plans nor the taking of any other action in accordance with this regulation is to be treated for the purposes of section 16 of the Act as the deposit of plans in accordance with building regulations.

Contravention of certain regulations not to be an offence

22. Regulation 17 is designated as a provision to which section 35 of the Act (penalty for contravening building regulations) does not apply.

Transitional provisions

23.- (1) Subject to paragraph (2), the Regulations specified in Schedule 3 shall continue to apply in relation to any building work as if these Regulations had not been made where-

(a) before 1st January 2001 a building notice, an initial notice, an amendment notice or a public body's notice has been given to, or full plans have been deposited with, a local authority; and

(b) building work is carried out or is to be carried out in accordance with any such notice or plans, whether with or without any departure from such plans.

(2) Where an initial notice given before 1st January 2001 is varied by an amendment notice given on or after that date, the Regulations specified in Schedule 3 shall continue to apply as if these Regulations had not been made, to so much of the building work as could have been carried out under that initial notice if the amendment notice had not been given.

Revocations

24. The Regulations specified in Schedule 3 are hereby revoked.

22   It is not an offence under section 35 of the Building Act if the local authority fail to give a completion certificate in accordance with Regulation 17.

23   Where a building notice, an initial notice, an amendment notice or a public body's notice was given, or full plans were deposited before 1st January 2001 the work continues to be subject to the Regulations specified in Schedule 3 of the Building Regulations 2000. Where a building notice was given or plans were deposited on or after that date the 2000 Regulations (and the subsequent amendments) apply, subject, in the case of the amendments, to their own transitional provisions. The transitional provisions for the Building (Amendment) Regulations 2001 are explained in DTLR Circular 03/2001.

SCHEDULE 1 – REQUIREMENTS

Regulations 4 and 6

Requirement	*Limits on application*

PART A STRUCTURE

Loading

A1.- (1) The building shall be constructed so that the combined dead, imposed and wind loads are sustained and transmitted by it to the ground-

    (a)   safely; and

    (b)   without causing such deflection or deformation of any part of the building, or such movement of the ground, as will impair the stability of any part of another building.

(2) In assessing whether a building complies with sub-paragraph (1) regard shall be had to the imposed and wind loads to which it is likely to be subjected in the ordinary course of its use for the purpose for which it is intended.

Ground movement

A2. The building shall be constructed so that ground movement caused by-

    (a)   swelling, shrinkage or freezing of the subsoil; or

    (b)   landslip or subsidence (other than subsidence arising from shrinkage), in so far as the risk can be reasonably foreseen, will not impair the stability of any part of the building.

Disproportionate collapse

A3. The building shall be constructed so that in the event of an accident the building will not suffer collapse to an extent disproportionate to the cause.

Requirement A3 applies only to a building having five or more storeys (each basement level being counted as one storey) excluding a storey within the roof space where the slope of the roof does not exceed 70° to the horizontal.

A1/2   Sections 1 to 4 of Approved Document A1/2 cover the requirements of A1 and A2 and give guidance on:

the sizing of structural elements for certain residential buildings no greater than three storeys in height (and other small buildings) of traditional construction;

the support and fixing of external wall cladding;

the re-covering of roofs where this is considered to be a material alteration;

various codes and standards for structural design and construction which are relevant to all building types.

Additionally, information sources are included regarding landslip and the structural appraisal of existing buildings subject to a change of use.

Paragraph A3 requires that a building with five or more storeys does not suffer from a large scale collapse as a result of an accident in a part of the building. The extent of any collapse should be commensurate with the scale of the incident which caused the collapse. When counting the number of storeys, include basements but exclude rooms in the roof space where the pitch of the roof is less than 70° to the horizontal.

A3   The guidance given in Approved Document A3 deals with a number of ways of reducing the sensitivity of the building to disproportionate collapse in the event of an accident. Part A and Approved Document A are currently under review.

Requirement	*Limits on application*

PART B FIRE SAFETY

Means of warning and escape

B1. The building shall be designed and constructed so that there are appropriate provisions for the early warning of fire, and appropriate means of escape in case of fire from the building to place of safety outside the building capable of being safely and effectively used at all material times.

Requirement B1 does not apply to any prison provided under section 33 of the Prisons Act 1952 (power to provide prisons etc.).

Internal fire spread (linings)

B2.- (1) To inhibit the spread of fire within the building the internal linings shall-

(a) adequately resist the spread of flame over their surfaces; and

(b) have, if ignited, a rate of heat release which is reasonable in the circumstances.

(2) In this paragraph "internal linings" mean the materials lining any partition, wall, ceiling or other internal structure.

Internal fire spread (structure)

B3.- (1) The building shall be designed and constructed so that, in the event of a fire, its stability will be maintained for a reasonable period.

(2) A wall common to two or more buildings shall be designed and constructed so that it adequately resists the spread of fire between those buildings. For the purposes of this sub-paragraph a house in a terrace and a semi-detached house are each to be treated as a separate building.

(3) To inhibit the spread of fire within the building, it shall be sub-divided with fire-resisting construction to an extent appropriate to the size and intended use of the building.

Requirement B3(3) does not apply to material alterations to any prison provided under section 33 of the Prisons Act 1952.

(4) The building shall be designed and constructed so that the unseen spread of fire and smoke within concealed spaces in its structure and fabric is inhibited.

Part B (Fire safety) aims to ensure the safety of the occupants and of others who may be affected by a building, and to provide assistance for fire fighters in the saving of lives.

Therefore, buildings must be constructed so that if a fire occurs:
the occupants are given suitable warning and are able to escape to a safe place away from the effects of the fire, fire spread over the internal linings of the walls and ceilings is inhibited, the stability is maintained for a sufficient period of time to allow evacuation of the occupants and access for fire fighting, fire spread within the building and from one building to another is kept to a minimum, and satisfactory access and facilities are provided for fire fighters.

B1   Paragraph B1 applies to all building types (except prisons). There may be other legislation which affects the means of escape in a building, particularly in Inner London under the Building Acts. This is reviewed in Section 4 of this Manual.

Approved Document B gives specific guidance on the design of means of warning and escape for dwellings (houses, flats and maisonettes). Other building types are dealt with by reference to general principles which address means of giving warning, and horizontal and vertical escape. Guidance is also given on lighting of escape routes, the provision of exit signs, the fire protection of lift installations, the performance of mechanical ventilation and air conditioning systems in the event of fire and the construction and siting of refuse chutes.

B2   Approved Document B gives guidance on the choice of lining materials for walls and ceilings. It concentrates on two properties of linings which influence fire spread (the rate of fire spread over the surface of a material when it is subject to intense radiant heating, and the rate at which the lining material gives off heat when burning) and gives guidance on how these properties can be controlled, mainly by restricting the use of certain materials.

B3   Guidance on the requirements of paragraph B3 is given in Approved Document B. It covers: measures to ensure that the load bearing elements of the structure of a building remain stable for an appropriate period of time during a fire, subdivision of the building into compartments by fire-resisting construction such as walls and floors, the sealing and subdivision of concealed spaces in the construction to inhibit the unseen spread of fire and smoke, the protection of openings and fire-stopping in compartment walls and floors, and special measures applying to car parks and shopping complexes.

Requirement	Limits on application

External fire spread

B4.- (1) The external walls of the building shall adequately resist the spread of fire over the walls and from one building to another, having regard to the height, use and position of the building.

(2) The roof of the building shall adequately resist the spread of fire over the roof and from one building to another, having regard to the use and position of the building.

Access and facilities for the fire service

B5.- (1) The building shall be designed and constructed so as to provide reasonable facilities to assist fire fighters in the protection of life.

(2) Reasonable provision shall be made within the site of the building to enable fire appliances to gain access to the building.

PART C SITE PREPARATION AND RESISTANCE TO MOISTURE

Preparation of site

C1. The ground to be covered by the building shall be reasonably free from vegetable matter.

Dangerous and offensive substances

C2. Reasonable precautions shall be taken to avoid danger to health and safety caused by substances found on or in the ground to be covered by the building.

Subsoil drainage

C3. Adequate subsoil drainage shall be provided if it is needed to avoid-

(a) the passage of ground moisture to the interior of the building;

(b) damage to the fabric of the building.

EXPLANATORY NOTES

B4 The guidance in Approved Document B is concerned with limiting the possible spread of fire between buildings. It does this by:
making provisions for the fire resistance of external walls and by limiting the susceptibility of their external surfaces to ignition and fire spread, limiting the extent of openings and other unprotected areas in external walls in relation to the space separation from the boundary of the site, and making provisions for reducing the risk of fire spread between roofs and over roof surfaces.

B5 Approved Document B deals with guidance on measures to assist the fire service, which are required by paragraph B5 of Schedule 1.

Guidance is given on the installation of fire mains within the building, the provision of vehicle access for high reach and pumping appliances, access for fire service personnel into and within the building and on the venting of heat and smoke from basements.

Generally, many of the provisions in Approved Document B are set out in terms of performance under standard test methods. The performance may be related to the use and size of the building, and in the case of B4 the distance of the wall or roof from the boundary of the site. Appendix A of the document sets out different ways that this performance can be shown to be achieved.

Paragraphs C1 and C2 of Schedule 1 apply to the area of ground covered by the building. C3 applies more generally to require subsoil drainage of the site.

C1/3 Guidance on paragraphs C1 and C3 is included in Section 1 of Approved Document C.

The need to remove vegetable matter, such as turf from the site of a building does not apply to some storage buildings in which the operatives are employed only in goods handling or in buildings where the removal would not serve to increase the health and safety of the users.

C2 Section 2 of Approved Document C gives guidance on the actions to be taken in dealing with contaminants encountered in the ground to be covered by the building.

Contaminants include any material in or on the ground to be covered by the building (including faecal or animal matter) and any substance which is, or could become: toxic, corrosive, explosive, flammable or radioactive. Therefore it includes the naturally occuring radioactive gas radon and gases produced by landfill sites, such as carbon dioxide and methane.

Further information is available in: *Radon: guidance on protective measures for new dwellings*, BR 211, 3rd edition 1999, and *Construction of new buildings on gas contaminated land*, BR212.

Both are available from CRC Ltd, 151 Rosebery Avenue, London, EC1R 4GB

C1/3 It may not always be necessary to drain the site of a building if the building can be designed and constructed to prevent the passage of ground and surface water to the inside or to materials which might be adversely affected by it.

Requirement	*Limits on application*

Resistance to weather and ground moisture

C4. The walls, floors and roof of the building shall adequately resist the passage of moisture to the inside of the building.

PART D TOXIC SUBSTANCES

Cavity insulation

D1. If insulating material is inserted into a cavity in a cavity wall reasonable precautions shall be taken to prevent the subsequent permeation of any toxic fumes from that material into any part of the building occupied by people.

PART E RESISTANCE TO THE PASSAGE OF SOUND

Airborne sound (walls)

E1. A wall which-

    (a) separates a dwelling from another building or from another dwelling, or

    (b) separates a habitable room or kitchen within a dwelling from another part of the same building which is not used exclusively as part of the dwelling,

shall resist the transmission of airborne sound.

Airborne sound (floors and stairs)

E2. A floor or stair which separates a dwelling from another dwelling, or from another part of the same building which is not used exclusively as part of the dwelling, shall have reasonable resistance to the transmission of airborne sound.

Impact sound (floors and stairs)

E3. A floor or stair above a dwelling which separates it from another dwelling, or from another part of the same building which is not used exclusively as part of the dwelling, shall have reasonable resistance to the transmission of impact sound.

C4   Section 3 of the Approved Document gives guidance on resistance to weather and ground moisture for the walls, floors and roof of the building.

Where the interior of the building is normally so moisture-laden that any increase will not affect the health of the people in it, the Approved Document recognises that 'no provision' may be adequate for walls and floors next to the ground as regards this requirement.

See also D1 for guidance on cavity insulation.

Part C and Approved Document C are currently under review.

D1   Filling a cavity wall, whether new or existing, with insulating material is building work to which the Regulations apply. Paragraph D1 of Schedule 1 is aimed specifically at cavity fill materials such as urea-formaldehyde foam which might cause toxic fumes to be released into the building as they cure.

See also C4 for guidance on resistance to moisture penetration in cavity walls, and L1 and L2 for guidance on the selection of insulating materials for the purposes of conserving fuel and power.

The requirements of Part E apply to protect the occupants of dwellings (houses, flats and maisonettes) from noise generated in adjoining dwellings or other buildings, but this does not include control over sound entering a dwelling through the external walls.

E1/2/3   The Approved Document describes and illustrates some wall and floor constructions which provide an acceptable reduction in the transmission of sound for both new work and conversions. It includes guidance on testing a construction which differs from the examples illustrated, to provide evidence for it to be replicated. It also gives guidance on limited use of laboratory tests.

It should be noted that the requirements for resistance to airborne and impact sound for floors also include stairs where they form part of the separating element between dwellings.

The effect of this regulation is that where, for example, a floor separates a dwelling above from a shop below, no action need be taken to control impact sound.

Part E and Approved Document E are currently under review.

Requirement	*Limits on application*

PART F VENTILATION

Means of ventilation

F1.   There shall be adequate means of ventilation provided for people in the building.   Requirement F1 does not apply to a building or space within a building_

    (a)   into which people do not normally go; or

    (b)   which is used solely for storage; or

    (c)   which is a garage used solely in connection with a single dwelling.

Condensation in roofs

F2.   Adequate provision shall be made to prevent excessive condensation-

    (a)   in a roof; or

    (b)   in a roof void above an insulated ceiling.

PART G HYGIENE

Sanitary conveniences and washing facilities

G1. (1)   Adequate sanitary conveniences shall be provided in rooms provided for that purpose, or in bathrooms. Any such room or bathroom shall be separated from places where food is prepared.

    (2)   Adequate washbasins shall be provided in-

        (a)   rooms containing water closets; or

        (b)   rooms or spaces adjacent to rooms containing water closets.

         Any such room or space shall be separated from places where food is prepared.

    (3)   There shall be a suitable installation for the provision of hot and cold water to wash basins provided in accordance with paragraph (2)

    (4)   Sanitary coveniences and washbasins to which this paragraph applies shall be designed and installed so as to allow effective cleaning.

The provisions in the Approved Document for requirement F1 would, if followed, prevent the service of an improvement notice with regard to the requirements for ventilation in regulation 6(1) of the Workplace (Health, Safety and Welfare) Regulations 1992. The requirement may be met if ventilation is provided which under normal conditions is capable (if used) of restricting the accumulation of such moisture (which could lead to mould growth) and pollutants originating within a building as would otherwise become a hazard to the health of the people in the building.

F1   Approved Document F gives guidance on: dispersal of water vapour and extraction where this is produced in significant quantities (eg kitchens, bathrooms and utility rooms), extraction of pollutants which are a danger to health, from areas where they are produced in significant quantities (eg rest rooms where smoking is permitted), rapid dilution of water vapour and pollutants (usually by providing openable windows),background ventilation to provide a minimum supply of fresh air over long periods, and the air supply through mechanical ventilation and air conditioning systems for non-domestic buildings where these are proposed.

Reference should also be made to Approved Document B for guidance on the design of mechanical ventilation and air conditioning systems for the purpose of fire safety, and Approved Document J in relation to the provision for combustion air to appliances.

F2   In a roof space and in the spaces above insulated ceilings there is a risk that condensation will form in the space above the insulation. The guidance in Approved Document F is aimed at limiting condensation so that the thermal performance of the insulating material, and the structural performance of the roof construction, will not be substantially and permanently reduced.

Further detailed guidance is given in the BRE report BR 262 Thermal insulation: avoiding risks.

G1   The requirement in paragraph G1 of Schedule 1 replaces section 26 of the Building Act 1984.

The Approved Document gives guidance on the scale of provision of sanitary conveniences and washing facilities in dwellings (houses, flats, and maisonettes) and houses in multiple occupation. For other building types reference is made to other relevant legislation. The reference in the current (1992) edition of the Approved Document to regulations made under the *Offices, Shops and Railway Premises Act 1963 and the Factories Act 1961* should be ignored since both have been replaced by recommendations contained in the *Workplace (Health, Safety and Welfare) Regulations 1992*. Reference should also be made, as appropriate, to the Food Hygiene (General) Regulations 1970 (as amended by the *Food Hygiene (Amendment Regulations 1990)* (which apply to premises used for the purposes of a food business) and to Part M of Schedule 1 (Access and facilities for disabled people).

Requirement	Limits on application

Bathrooms

G2. A bathroom shall be provided containing either a fixed bath or shower bath, and there shall be a suitable installation for the provision of hot and cold water to the bath or shower bath.

Requirement G2 applies only to dwellings.

Hot water storage

G3. A hot water storage system that has a hot water storage vessel which does not incorporate a vent pipe to the atmosphere shall be installed by a person competent to do so, and there shall be precautions-

(a) to prevent the temperature of the stored water at any time exceeding 100°C; and

(b) to ensure that the hot water discharged from safety devices is safely conveyed to where it is visible but will not cause danger to persons in or about the building.

Requirement G3 does not apply to-

(a) a hot water storage system that has a storage vessel with a capacity of 15 litres or less;

(b) a system providing space heating only;

(c) a system which heats or stores water for the purposes only of an industrial process.

PART H DRAINAGE AND WASTE DISPOSAL

Foul water drainage

H1.- (1) An adequate system of drainage shall be provided to carry foul water from appliances within the building to one of the following, listed in order of priority:

(a) a public sewer; or, where that is not reasonably practicable,

(b) a private sewer communicating with a public sewer; or, where that is not reasonably practicable,

(c) either a septic tank which has an appropriate form of secondary treatment or another wastewater treatment system; or, where that is not reasonably practicable,

(d) a cesspool.

Requirement H1 does not apply to the diversion of water which has been used for personal washing or for the washing of clothes, linen or other articles to collection systems for reuse.

The requirement in paragraph G2 of Schedule 1 replaces section 27 of the Building Act 1984.

G2   The Approved Document recommends that the same provision for a bathroom applies also to a house in multiple occupation.

G3   The Approved Document recommends that such a system should be the subject of an agreed method of approval or assessment and should be installed by a competent person. It must also comply with the Water Supply (Water Fittings) Regulations 1999.

The requirement in paragraph H1 of Schedule 1 replaces paragraphs (1) and (2) of section 21 (Provision of drainage) of the Building Act 1984. However, a local authority retain their powers under paragraph (4) to require connection to a sewer in certain specified circumstances. Any questions arising between the local authority and the person by whom, or on whose behalf, plans are deposited as to the necessity to connect to a sewer may be decided by a magistrates' court.

The Water Undertaker may require preliminary treatment of trade effluent before it can be discharged into a public sewer. 'Sanitary convenience' is not defined in Part H although it is defined as a closet or urinal in Approved Document G.

H1   Approved Document H gives guidance on the design of above ground sanitary pipework and below ground foul drainage. It stresses the need for the drainage system to be designed and constructed to:
convey foul water to a suitable outfall (a foul or combined sewer, cesspool, septic tank or holding tank),
minimise the risk of blockage or leakage,
prevent the entry of foul air into the building under normal working conditions,
be ventilated, and accessible for clearing blockages and
not increase the vulnerability of the building to flooding.

See also: Water Industry Act 1991, s.94 (duty of water undertaker to provide public sewers); Water Industry Act 1991, ss.106 to 108 (rights of owners and occupiers of premises to connect to a public sewer); and the Building Act 1984, s.22 (drainage of buildings in combination).

Sewers (ie. a drain serving more than one property) should normally have a minimum diameter of 100mm when serving no more than 10 dwellings . Sewers serving more than 10 dwellings should normally have a minimum diameter of 150mm. Access points to sewers should be in places where they are accessible and apparent for use in an emergency.

Requirement	Limits on application

(2) In this Part "foul water" means waste water which comprises or includes -

(a) waste from a sanitary convenience, a bidet or an appliance used for washing receptacles for foul waste;

(b) water which has been used for food preparation, cooking or washing.

Wastewater treatment systems and cesspools

H2.- (1) Any septic tank and its form of secondary treatment, other wastewater treatment system or cesspool shall be so sited and constructed that -

(a) it is not prejudicial to the health of any person;

(b) it will not contaminate any watercourse, underground water or water supply;

(c) there are adequate means of access for emptying and maintenance, and

(d) where relevant, it will function to a sufficient standard for the protection of health in the event of a power failure.

(2) Any septic tank, holding tank which is part of a wastewater treatment system or cesspool, shall be -

(a) of adequate capacity;

(b) so constructed that it is impermeable to liquids; and

(c) adequately ventilated.

(3) Where a foul drainage system from a building discharges to a septic tank, wastewater treatment system, or cesspool, a durable notice shall be affixed in a suitable place in the building containing information on any continuing maintenance required to avoid risks to health.

Wastewater treatment systems should only be considered where the nature of the subsoil indicates that the operation of the system and the quality and method of disposal of the effluent will be satisfactory and where connection to mains drainage is not practicable. The requirements in the Regulations are concerned with siting, construction, capacity, ventilation and the provision of maintenance information. The quality of the discharged effluent is not the subject of the Building Regulations but some installations may require a consent for discharge from the Environment Agency.

Local authorities have powers under the Public Health Act 1936, s 48 to test wastewater treatment systems or cesspools that they consider to be defective and under s 50 to require a person to carry out repairs or periodically empty the tank if they have caused or allowed the tank to leak or overflow. Similar powers exist under s 59 of the Building Act 1984 where a wastewater treatment system or cesspool is deemed to be insufficient, in poor condition or defective.

Additionally, the Environment Agency may take action against any person who knowingly permits pollution of a stream, river, lake etc. or groundwater, by requiring them to carry out works to prevent the pollution (Water Resources Act 1991 (as amended), s 161A).

H2 The Approved Document deals with the siting, construction and capacity of wastewater treatment systems and cesspools so that:

they are not prejudicial to health or a nuisance,

they do not adversely affect water sources or resources,

they do not pollute controlled waters, and

they are not sited in an area where there is a risk of flooding.

They should be adequately ventilated and should be constructed so that the leakage of the contents and the ingress of subsoil water is prevented.

The 2002 edition of Approved Document H contains guidance, for the first time on: the siting and construction of drainage fields, and the provision of information regarding the nature and frequency of the maintenance needs of wastewater systems and cesspools.

Requirement	Limits on application

Rainwater drainage

H3.- (1) Adequate provision shall be made for rainwater to be carried from the roof of the building.

(2) Paved areas around the building shall be so constructed as to be adequately drained.

Requirement H3(2) applies only to paved areas:

(a) which provide access to the building pursuant to paragraph M2 of Schedule 1 (access for disabled people);

(b) which provide access to or from a place of storage pursuant to paragraph H6(2) of Schedule 1 (solid waste storage); or

(c) in any passage giving access to the building, where this is intended to be used in common by the occupiers of two or more other buildings.

(3) Rainwater from a system provided pursuant to sub-paragraphs (1) or (2) shall discharge to one of the following listed in order of priority-

Requirement H3(3) does not apply to the gathering of rainwater for reuse.

(a) an adequate soakaway or some other adequate infiltration system; or, where that is not reasonably practicable,

(b) a watercourse; or, where that is not reasonably practicable,

(c) a sewer

Building over sewers

H4.- (1) The erection or extension of a building or work involving the underpinning of a building shall be carried out in a way that is not detrimental to the building, building extension or to the continued maintenance of the drain, sewer or disposal main.

Requirement H4 applies only to work carried out -

(a) over a drain, sewer or disposal main, that is shown on any map of sewers; or

(b) on any such site or in such a manner as would result in interference with the use of, or obstruction of the access of any person to, any drain, sewer or disposal main which is shown on any map of sewers.

(2) In this paragraph "disposal main" means any pipe, tunnel or conduit used for the conveyance of effluent to or from a sewage disposal works, which is not a public sewer.

(3) In this paragraph and paragraph H5 "map of sewers" means any records kept by a sewerage undertaker under Section 199 of the Water Industry Act 1991.

Section 60 of the Building Act 1984 prevents the use of rainwater pipes for conveying soil or drainage from a sanitary convenience or for being used as a ventilating shaft to a drain or sewer conveying foul water. See also the notes to H1 above.

H3   Approved Document H gives guidance on the need for rainwater from roofs and paved areas to be carried away either by a drainage system or by some other means. (such as an eaves drop system).

Where provided, a rainwater drainage system should:

carry the flow of rainwater from the roof to a suitable outfall (a surface water or combined sewer, soakaway or watercourse).

minimise the risk of blockage or leakage, and

be accessible for clearing blockages.

The Approved Document contains new guidance on the following:

precautions to be taken where rainwater is permitted to soak into the ground,

siphonic roof drainage systems,

eaves drop systems,

rainwater recovery systems,

drainage of paved areas,

the design of soakaways and other infiltration drainage systems, and

the use of oil separators.

The requirement in paragraph H4 of Schedule 1 replaces section 18 of the Building Act 1984.

H4   The Approved Document gives guidance on the construction, extension or underpinning of a building over or within 3m of the centreline of an existing drain, sewer or disposal main shown on the Sewerage Undertaker's sewer records whether or not that sewer is a public sewer.

Building work should be carried out so that:

it will not cause overloading or damage to the drain, sewer or disposal main, and it will not obstruct reasonable access to any manhole or inspection chamber.

Future maintenance works to the drain, sewer or disposal main must be possible without undue obstruction, and the risk of damage to the building must not be excessive due to failure of the drain, sewer or disposal main.

The guidance explains that precautions should be taken if piles are to be placed close to drains.

Requirement	*Limits on application*

Separate systems of drainage

H5. Any systems for discharging water to a sewer which is provided pursuant to paragraph H3 shall be separate from that provided for the conveyance of foul water from the building.

Requirement H5 applies only to a system provided in connection with the erection or extension of a building where it is reasonably practicable for the system to discharge directly or indirectly to a sewer for the separate conveyance of surface water which is-

(a) shown on a map of sewers; or

(b) under construction either by the sewerage undertaker or some other person (where the sewer is the subject of an agreement to make a declaration of vesting pursuant to section 104 of the Water Act 1991).

Solid waste storage

H6.- (1) Adequate provision shall be made for storage of solid waste.

(2) Adequate means of access shall be provided-

    (a) for people in the building to the place of storage; and

    (b) from the place of storage to a collection point (where one has been specified by the waste collection authority under section 46 (household,waste) or section 47 (commercial waste) of the Environmental Protection Act 1990) or to a street (where no collection point has been specified).

PART J COMBUSTION APPLIANCES AND FUEL STORAGE SYSTEMS

Air supply

J1. Combustion appliances shall be so installed that there is an adequate supply of air to them for combustion, to prevent overheating and for the efficient working of any flue.

Requirements J1, J2 and J3 apply only to fixed combustion appliances (including incinerators).

Discharge of products of combustion

J2. Combustion appliances shall have adequate provision for the discharge of the products of combustion to the outside air.

H5 The guidance in Approved Document H is designed to ensure that:

rainwater does not enter the public foul sewer system, (where it can cause over-loading and flooding), rainwater does not enter a wastewater treatment system or cesspool not designed to take rainwater where it might cause pollution by overloading the capacity of the system or cesspool (and in the case of cesspools, lead to excessive maintenance costs), and foul water including run-off from soiled or contaminated paved areas, does not enter the rainwater sewer system or an infiltration drainage system intended only for rainwater (where it can cause pollution).

This requirement replaces sections 23(1) and (2) of the Building Act 1984. Section 23(3) makes it an offence to close or obstruct the means of access by which refuse is removed from a building without the consent of the local authority.

H6 The Approved Document gives guidance on the design, siting and capacity of refuse containers and chutes for domestic developments.

For non-domestic developments it is recommended that the collecting authority is consulted regarding:

the volume and nature of the waste, and the storage capacity required, any requirements for segregation of waste for recycling, the method of storage, including any proposals for on-site treatment, the location of storage areas, treatment areas and waste collection points and the means of access to these, hygiene arrangements and fire hazards and protection measures.

Sections 45 to 47 of the Environmental Protection Act 1990 contain provisions with respect to the duties of waste collection authorities and their powers to require the provision of suitable waste receptacles (see Section 4 Other Legislation).

Section 73 of the Building Act 1984 gives a local authority special powers where a new building overreaches an adjacent chimney, (see Section 4 Other Legislation).

Requirements J1 to J3 apply only to fixed fuel-burning appliances and incinerators.

J1/2/3 The Approved Document for Part J gives advice on the amount of air supply needed for safe combustion of the fuel, the safe discharge of the products of combustion to the outside air so that they do not become a hazard to health, and measures to reduce the risk of people suffering burns or the building catching fire.

The guidance also includes ways of demonstrating that the safe performance of combustion installations is not undermined by mechanical extract ventilation systems. See also Part F (Requirement F1) for guidance on ventilation generally.

	Requirement	*Limits on application*

Protection of the building

J3. Combustion appliances and flue-pipes shall be so installed, and fire-places and chimneys shall be so constructed and installed, as to reduce to a reasonable level the risk of people suffering burns or the building catching fire in consequence of their use.

Provision of information

J4. Where a hearth, fireplace, flue or chimney is provided or extended, a durable notice containing information on the performance capabilities of the hearth, fireplace, flue or chimney shall be affixed in a suitable place in the building for the purpose of enabling combustion appliances to be safely installed.

Protection of liquid fuel storage systems

J5. Liquid fuel storage systems and the pipes connecting them to combustion appliances shall be so constructed and separated from buildings and the boundary of the premises as to reduce to a reasonable level the risk of the fuel igniting in the event of fire in adjacent buildings or premises.

Requirement J5 applies only to -

(a) fixed oil storage tanks with capacities greater than 90 litres and connecting pipes; and

(b) fixed liquified petroleum gas storage installations with capacities greater than 150 litres and connecting pipes,

which are located outside the building and which serve combustion appliances (including incinerators) in the building.

Protection against pollution

J6. Oil storage tanks and the pipes connecting them to combustion appliances shall-

(a) be so constructed and protected as to reduce to a reasonable level the risk of the oil escaping and causing pollution; and

(b) have affixed in a prominent position a durable notice containing information on how to respond to an oil escape so as to reduce to a reasonable level the risk of pollution.

Requirement J6 applies only to fixed oil storage tanks with capacities of 3,500 litres or less, and connecting pipes, which are -

(a) located outside the building; and

(b) serve fixed combustion appliances (including incinerators) in a building used wholly or mainly as a private dwelling,

but does not apply to buried systems.

J4   Paragraph J4 calls for a notice providing the performance characteristics of the hearth, fireplace, flue or chimney to be fixed in an appropriate place in the building.

The Approved Document gives guidance on the form, content and location of such notices where:

a hearth, fireplace recess or a fluebox has been newly built or refurbished, or

a flue has been newly built or relined.

The notice will contain information which is essential to the correct application and use of these facilities, such as:

their location and date of installation,

the category of the flue and generic types of appliances that can be safely connected to it,

the type and size of the flue (or liner if it has been relined) and the name of the manufacturer.

J5   The Approved Document gives guidance on the protection of oil and LPG fuel storage systems from fire. This includes the positioning and/or shielding, so as to protect these systems from fires that might occur in adjacent buildings or on adjacent property.

J6   J6 makes provision for protection against pollution of bore holes, water and drainage courses and for permanent labels containing information on how to respond to oil escapes, to be positioned in a prominent position. New guidance is given on assessing the risk of pollution and the necessary, reasonable measures to contain leaks.

Requirement	*Limits on application*

PART K PROTECTION FROM FALLING, COLLISION AND IMPACT

Stairs, ladders and ramps

K1. Stairs, ladders and ramps shall be so designed, constructed and installed as to be safe for people moving between different levels in or about the building.	Requirement K1 applies only to stairs, ladders and ramps which form part of the building.

Protection from falling

K2. (a) Any stairs, ramps, floors and balconies and any roof to which people have access, and	Requirement K2(a) applies only to stairs and ramps which form part of the building.
(b) any light well, basement area or similar sunken area connected to a building,	
shall be provided with barriers where it is necessary to protect people in or about the building from falling.	

Vehicle barriers and loading bays

K3. (1) Vehicle ramps and any levels in a building to which vehicles have access, shall be provided with barriers where it is necessary to protect people in or about the building.

(2) Vehicle loading bays shall be constructed in such a way, or be provided with such features, as may be necessary to protect people in them from collision with vehicles.

Protection from collision with open windows etc

K4. Provision shall be made to prevent people moving in or about the building from colliding with open windows, skylights or ventilators.	Requirement K4 does not apply to dwellings.

Protection against impact from and trapping by doors

K5. (1) Provision shall be made to prevent any door or gate-	Requirement K5 does not apply to:
(a) which slides or opens upwards, from falling onto any person; and	(a) dwellings, or
(b) which is powered, from trapping any person.	(b) any door or gate which is part of a lift.
(2) Provision shall be made for powered doors and gates to be opened in the event of power failure.	
(3) Provision shall be made to ensure a clear view of the space on either side of a swing door or gate.	

Compliance with Part K (and where appropriate M2 as it relates to stairs and ramps) of the Building Regulations, would prevent the service of an improvement notice with regard to the relevant requirements of the Workplace (Health, Safety and Welfare) Regulations 1992

K1   The Approved Document deals with the design, construction and installation of stairs, ladders and ramps. It shows that an acceptable level of safety can be achieved by different standards of provision, depending on the circumstances (eg in a public building the standard of provision may be higher than in a dwelling, to reflect the lesser familiarity and number of users).

K2/3   The Approved Document deals with:

the provision of guards designed to prevent pedestrians from falling, the provision of vehicle barriers capable of resisting or deflecting the impact of vehicles, and measures to protect people in loading bays from being struck or crushed by vehicles by providing adequate numbers of exits or refuges.

K4   The Approved Document includes guidance on the installation of windows, so that parts which project when the window is open are kept away from people in and around the building, and on the provision of features which guide people away from open windows, skylights and ventilators.

K5   The Approved Document describes measures which are designed to prevent the opening and closing of doors and gates from presenting a safety hazard. These include vision panels in doors and safety features to prevent people being trapped by doors and gates.

Reference should also be made to the recommendations for the design of stairs for means of escape included in Approved Document B (Fire safety) and to the recommendations for the design of stairs and ramps for use by disabled people in Approved Document M (Access and facilities for disabled people).

Requirement	*Limits on application*

PART L CONSERVATION OF FUEL AND POWER

Dwellings

L1.   Reasonable provision shall be made for the conservation of fuel and power in dwellings by-

(a)   limiting the heat loss:

    (i)   through the fabric of the building;

    (ii)   from hot water pipes and hot air ducts used for space heating;

    (iii)   from hot water vessels;

(b)   providing space heating and hot water systems which are energy-efficient;

(c)   providing lighting systems with appropriate lamps and sufficient controls so that the energy can be used efficiently;

                    The requirement for sufficient controls in paragraph L1(c) applies only to external lighting systems fixed to the building.

(d)   providing sufficient information with the heating and hot water services so that building occupiers can operate and maintain the services in such a manner as to use no more energy than is reasonable in the circumstances.

The Building (Amendment) Regulations 2001, S.I. 2001 No. 3335, have subdivided Part L of Schedule 1 into Part L1, covering dwellings, and Part L2 covering all other types of buildings. Two new Approved Documents (2002) reflect this subdivision.

Guidance on avoiding technical risks (such as rain penetration, condensation etc.) which might arise from the application of energy conservation measures, is given in BRE Report 262: *"Thermal insulation: avoiding risks"* (updated edition published by BRE and HMSO and available from The Stationery Office and CRC Ltd, November 2001 ISBN 1860815154).

L1   Information on the main changes to Approved Document L1 can be found on the inside of the front cover of the Approved Document.

Other features of the Approved Document include:
a new summary offered for use as a checklist for establishing compliance (see pages 5 and 6),
Section 0 – General, sets out the ground rules and lists what the Secretary of State considers to be reasonable provisions/approaches to meeting the requirements,
Section 1 – Design and construction, gives details of alternative methods of showing compliance,
Section 2 – Work on existing dwellings, includes guidance on reasonable provision for replacement windows and boilers and for work in historic buildings.

L1(a)   The SAP rating for each new dwelling must still be calculated and given to the local authority in accordance with requirement 16 of the Regulations or to the Approved Inspector in accordance with regulation 12 of the Approved Inspectors Regulations. However, it can no longer be used as a means of showing compliance in its own right.

Guidance on ways of limiting heat losses due to thermal bridging at junctions and around openings, and through unwanted air leakage is given in the Approved Document by reference to the following BRE publications – *Limiting thermal bridging and air leakage: Robust construction details for dwellings and similar buildings*, TSO, 2001, and BRE IP 17/01 *Assessing the effects of thermal bridging at junctions and around openings in the external elements of buildings*, CRC Ltd. Both are available from The Stationery Office or CRC Ltd.

L1(d)   Heating and hot water systems need to be commissioned and provided with User Manuals. The Approved Document indicates that Building Control Bodies can accept self-certification of compliance and offers the commissioning certificate published as part of the Benchmark Code of Practice for the Installation and Servicing of Central Heating Systems (administered by the Central Heating Council, tel: 01926 423284) as a suitable example.

The Approved Document contains the following Appendices:
A – contains building element U-values in a series of look-up tables
B – deals with the calculation of U-values generally, using the combined method
C – deals with the calculation of U-values for ground floors
D – shows how to determine the U-values for windows, doors and rooflights in the elemental method
E – shows how to apply the Target U-value method of showing compliance. This is the method most likely to be used by volume house builders
F – gives examples of typical SAP ratings and carbon indexes for a range of dwelling designs
G – gives a worksheet for calculating the carbon index of a dwelling

Requirement	Limits on application

Buildings other than dwellings

L2. Reasonable provision shall be made for the conservation of fuel and power in buildings other than dwellings by-

(a) limiting the heat losses and gains through the fabric of the building;

(b) limiting the heat loss:

    (i) from hot water pipes and hot air ducts used for space heating;

    (ii) from hot water vessels and hot water service pipes;

(c) providing space heating and hot water systems which are energy-efficient;

(d) limiting exposure to solar overheating;

(e) making provision where air conditioning and mechanical ventilation systems are installed, so that no more energy needs to be used than is reasonable in the circumstances;

               Requirements L2(e) and (f) apply only within buildings where more than 200m² of floor area is to be served by air conditioning or mechanical ventilation systems.

(f) limiting the heat gains by chilled water and refrigerant vessels and pipes and air ducts that serve air conditioning systems;

(g) providing lighting systems which are energy-efficient;

               Requirement L2(g) applies only within buildings and parts of buildings where more than 100 m² of floor area is to be served by artificial lighting.

(h) providing sufficient information with the relevant services so that the building can be operated and maintained in such a manner as to use no more energy than is reasonable in the circumstances.

L2 Information on the main changes to Approved Document L2 can be found on the inside of the front cover of the Approved Document.

Other features of the Approved Document include:

a new summary offered for use as a checklist for establishing compliance (see pages 5 to 7),
Section 0 – General, sets out the ground rules and lists what the Secretary of State considers to be reasonable provisions/approaches to meeting the requirements,
Section 1 – Design, gives details of alternative methods of showing compliance and offers alternative ways of showing how air leakage standards may be met and how solar overheating may be avoided.
Section 2 – Construction, offers insulation continuity thermography and air pressure testing as options which can be used to show compliance but it is expected that designers and contractors will prefer to use the new robust details.
Section 3 – Providing information, deals with the content of building log-books and the installation of energy meters.
Section 4 – Work on existing buildings, includes guidance on reasonable provision for replacement windows, heating and hot water systems, lighting systems, and air conditioning or mechanical ventilation systems. Guidance is also given on the reasonable provision for work in historic buildings.

The Approved Document contains the following Appendices:
A – contains building element U-values in a series of look-up tables
B – deals with the calculation of U-values generally, using the combined method
C – deals with the calculation of U-values for ground floors
D – shows how to determine the U-values for windows, doors and rooflights in the elemental method
E – shows how to carry out trade-off calculations between construction elements, and between construction elements and heating system efficiency
F – gives examples of ways of meeting the luminaire efficacy requirement for lighting installations
G – deals with the performance assessment method for office buildings and shows how to assess the contribution to carbon emissions due to building services design and operation
H – provides a way of showing compliance with the solar overheating requirement by means of a calculation of solar load.

Requirement	Limits on application

PART M ACCESS AND FACILITIES FOR DISABLED PEOPLE

Interpretation

M1. In this Part "disabled people" means people who have-

(a) an impairment which limits their ability to walk or which requires them to use a wheelchair for mobility, or

(b) impaired hearing or sight.

The requirements of Part M do not apply to-

(a) a material alteration;

(b) an extension to a dwelling, or any other extension which does not include a ground storey;

(c) any part of a building which is used solely to enable the building or any service or fitting in the building to be inspected, repaired or maintained.

Access and use

M2. Reasonable provision shall be made for disabled people to gain access to and to use the building.

Sanitary conveniences

M3.- (1) reasonable provision shall be made in the entrance storey of a dwelling for sanitary conveniences, or where the entrance storey contains no habitable rooms, reasonable provision for sanitary conveniences shall be made in either the entrance storey or a principal storey.

(2) In this paragraph "entrance storey" means the storey which contains the principal entrance to the dwelling, and "principal storey" means the storey nearest to the entrance storey which contains a habitable room, or if there are two such storeys equally near, either such storey.

(3) If sanitary conveniences are provided in any building which is not a dwelling, reasonable provision shall be made to accommodate disabled people.

Audience or spectator seating

M4. If the building contains audience or spectator seating, reasonable provision shall be made to accommodate disabled people.

2. Part M4 does not apply to dwellings

Part M is referred to in Regulation 3(3) as one of the parts of Schedule 1 which gives rise to a material alteration. However, when a building is altered there is no obligation to improve access and facilities for disabled people provided that the level of provision after alteration is not made any worse. Facilities may be moved but their suitability and access to them should not be reduced. Part M is under revision.

M1/2/3   The Approved Document for Part M covers:

access to the main entrances to the building from the edge of the site and from car parking within the curtilage,

access into and within the building and from one building to another on a site,

access to and use of the building's facilities,

design of the building's elements so that they are not a hazard to disabled people,

the provision and design of sanitary accommodation,

the provision and design of accommodation for disabled people in audience or spectator seating, and

aids for communication for people with impaired hearing or sight in auditoria, meeting rooms, reception areas and ticket offices.

Compliance with Building Regulation requirement M2 (in conjunction with Part K) where it relates to stairs and ramps, would prevent the service of an improvement notice with regard to the corresponding requirements of Regulation 17 of the Workplace (Health, Safety and Welfare) Regulations 1992.

The provisions in Approved Document M for dwellings, are intended to make it reasonably safe and convenient for disabled people to visit new dwellings and to use the principal storey. The provisions are expected to enable occupants to cope better with reducing mobility and to "stay put" longer in their own homes, although not necessarily to facilitate fully independent living for all disabled people.

The provisions should enable disabled people:

(a)   to reach the principal, or suitable alternative, entrance to the dwelling from the point of access;

(b)   to gain access to the principal storey of the dwelling; and

(c)   to have access to sanitary accommodation in a storey no higher than the principal storey.

Requirement	*Limits on application*

PART N GLAZING - SAFETY IN RELATION TO IMPACT, OPENING AND CLEANING

Protection against impact

N1. Glazing, with which people are likely to come into contact whilst moving in or about the building, shall-

    (a)   if broken on impact, break in a way which is unlikely to cause injury; or

    (b)   resist impact without breaking; or

    (c)   be shielded or protected from impact.

Manifestation of glazing

N2. Transparent glazing, with which people are likely to come into contact while moving in or about the building, shall incorporate features which make it apparent.

        Requirement N2 does not apply to dwellings.

Safe opening and closing of windows etc

N3. Windows, skylights and ventilators which can be opened by people in or about the building shall be so constructed or equipped that they may be opened, closed or adjusted safely.

        Requirement N3 does not apply to dwellings.

Safe access for cleaning windows etc

N4. Provision shall be made for any windows, skylights, or any transparent or translucent walls, ceilings or roofs to be safely accessible for cleaning.

        Requirement N4 does not apply to:

    (a)   dwellings, or

    (b)   any transparent or translucent elements whose surfaces are not intended to be cleaned.

N1 Glazing which is installed in a location where there was none previously as part of the erection, extension or material alteration of a building, other than an exempt building (see Schedule 2), is building work as defined by Regulation 3 and is subject to the requirements of Part N. A conservatory or porch having a floor area not exceeding 30m² is exempt under Class VII of Schedule 2 only where the glazing satisfies the requirements of Part N. Other glazing, such as replacement glazing, is not controlled, (but see Part L for replacement windows), but its supply may be subject to consumer protection legislation (see the General Product Safety Regulations 1994, S.I. 1994, No. 2328). People using buildings may come into contact with glazing in critical locations, such as, doors, door side panels and at low level in walls and partitions. The Approved Document describes measures which may be adopted to reduce the likelihood of cutting and piercing injuries occuring from contact with such glazing by making sure that it will break safely, be robust or be permanently protected.

N2 Approved Document N gives guidance on the measures that might be adopted to indicate the presence of large uninterrupted areas of transparent glazing with which people might collide. It does not apply to dwellings.

N3 Compliance with Building Regulation requirement N3 would prevent the service of an improvement notice with regard to the requirements for opening, closing or adjusting windows, skylights or ventilators in Regulation 15(1) of the Workplace (Health, Safety and Welfare) Regulations 1992.

The Approved Document provides guidance on the safe operation of openable windows, skylights and ventilators relating to the location of controls and the prevention of falling.

N4 Compliance with Building Regulation requirement N4 would prevent the service of an improvement notice with regard to the requirements for cleaning windows and skylights etc. in Regulation 16 of the Workplace (Health, Safety and Welfare) Regulations 1992.

Approved Document N4 is limited to providing guidance for safe means of access for cleaning glazed surfaces where there is danger of falling more than two metres.

Guidance is given on measures which can be adopted for safe cleaning, where the glazed surfaces cannot be reached from the ground, a floor or some other permanent stable surface.

Attention is also drawn to the following parts of the Regulations related to glazing:

Part B and Approved Document B (Fire safety) where guidance is included on fire resisting glazing and the reaction of glass to fire, and

Part K and Approved Document K (Protection from falling, collision and impact) for guidance on glazing which forms part of the protection from falling from one level to another, and which needs to ensure containment as well as limiting the risk of sustaining injury through contact.

Part L and Approved Document L for guidance on thermal performance.

SCHEDULE 2 – EXEMPT BUILDINGS AND WORK

Regulation 9

CLASS I

Buildings controlled under other legislation

1.   Any building the construction of which is subject to the Explosives Acts 1875 and 1923(a).

2.   Any building (other than a building containing a dwelling or a building used for office or canteen accommodation) erected on a site in respect of which a licence under the Nuclear Installations Act 1965(b) is for the time being in force.

3.   Any building included in the schedule of monuments maintained under section 1 of the Ancient Monuments and Archeological Areas Act 1979(c).

CLASS II

Buildings not frequented by people

A detached building–

(a)   into which people do not normally go; or

(b)   into which people go only intermittently and then only for the purpose of inspecting or maintaining fixed plant or machinery,

unless any point of such a building is less than one and a half times its height from

(i)   any point of a building into which people can or do normally go; or

(ii)   the nearest point of the boundary of the curtilage of that building, whichever is the nearer.

CLASS III

Greenhouses and agricultural buildings

1.   Subject to paragraph 3, a greenhouse.

2.   A building used, subject to paragraph 3, for agriculture, or a building principally for the keeping of animals, provided in each case that–

(a)   no part of the building is used as a dwelling;

(b)   no point of the building is less than one and a half times its height from any point of a building which contains sleeping accommodation; and

(c)   the building is provided with a fire exit which is not more than 30 metres from any point in the building.

3.   The descriptions of buildings in paragraphs 1 and 2 do not include a greenhouse or a building used for agriculture if the principal purpose for which they are used is retailing, packing or exhibiting.

4.   In paragraph 2, "agriculture" includes horticulture, fruit growing, the growing of plants for seed and fish farming.

CLASS IV

Temporary buildings

A building which is not intended to remain where it is erected for more than 28 days.

CLASS V

Ancillary buildings

1.   A building on a site, being a building which is intended to be used only in connection with the disposal of buildings or building plots on that site.

(a) 1875 c.17, 1923 c. 17
(b) 1965 c. 57, the only relevant amending instrument is SI 1974/2056
(c) 1979 c. 46

In general, The Building Regulations do not apply to the erection, extension or alteration of the buildings described in this schedule provided that they conform to the conditions listed opposite in each class (see regulation 9).

However, if work is carried out to an exempt building which would mean that it no longer came within the parameters listed in Schedule 2 then the Regulations would apply to that work. For example, if it was proposed to extend a small detached domestic garage so that its floor area would exceed $30m^2$ (see Class VI (1)), the work would be subject to control under the Regulations.

Additionally, if a building which falls into Classes I to VI has its use changed such that it would no longer fall within one of those classes, then the Regulations would apply by virtue of Regulation 5(f) to the change of use to the extent set out in Regulation 6.

2. A building on the site of construction or civil engineering works, which is intended to be used only during the course of those works and contains no sleeping accommodation.

3. A building, other than a building containing a dwelling or used as an office or showroom, erected for use on the site of and in connection with a mine or quarry.

CLASS VI

Small detached buildings

1. A detached single story building, having a floor area which does not exceed 30m², which contains no sleeping accommodation and is a building–

   (a) no point of which is less than one metre from the boundary of its curtilage; or

   (b) which is constructed substantially of non-combustible material.

2. A detached building designed and intended to shelter people from the effects of nuclear, chemical or conventional weapons, and not used for any other purpose, if–

   (a) its floor area does not exceed 30m²; and

   (b) the excavation for the building is no closer to any exposed part of another building or structure than a distance equal to the depth of the excavation plus one metre.

3. A detached building, having a floor area which does not exceed 15m², which contains no sleeping accommodation.

CLASS VII

Extensions

The extension of a building by the addition at ground level of–

   (a) a conservatory, porch, covered yard or covered way; or

   (b) a carport open on at least two sides;

where the floor area of that extension does not exceed 30m², provided that in the case of a conservatory or porch which is wholly or partly glazed, the glazing satisfies the requirements of Part N of Schedule 1.

The extensions listed in Class VII are exempt from control. However an extension which consists of a wholly or partly glazed conservatory or porch must have glazing which complies with Part N of Schedule 1.

The effect of this requirement is that it is not necessary to notify the local authority when constructing such a porch or conservatory provided that the glazing complies with Part N. If subsequently, it is found that the glazing does not comply, then the local authority may be able to take action for a contravention under section 36 of the Building Act 1984.

The term 'conservatory' is not defined in the Regulations. However, For the purposes of Part L (Conservation of fuel and power), Approved Document L1 (Conservation of fuel and power in dwellings) says in paragraph 1.58 - "a conservatory has not less than three-quarters of the area of its roof and not less than one-half of the area of its external walls made of translucent material."

SCHEDULE 3 – REVOCATION OF REGULATIONS

Regulation 24

Title	Reference
The Building Regulations 1991	SI 1991/2768
The Building Regulations (Amendment) Regulations 1992	SI 1992/1180
The Building Regulations (Amendment) Regulations 1994	SI 1994/1850
The Building Regulations (Amendment) Regulations 1995	SI 1995/1356
The Building Regulations (Amendment) Regulations 1997	SI 1997/1904
The Building Regulations (Amendment) Regulations 1998	SI 1998/2561
The Building Regulations (Amendment) Regulations 1999	SI 1999/77
The Building Regulations (Amendment) (No 2) Regulations 1999	SI 1999/3410
The Building Regulations (Amendment) Regulations 2000	SI 2000/1554

Section 4

OTHER LEGISLATION

Contents

Introduction

4.1   After consulting Section 1 of this Manual you may decide that The Building Regulations do not apply to your proposal. However, it may be the case that there is additional legislation which does apply. This section aims to give more information about legislation other than the Regulations which might affect your proposal. The information given is not a comprehensive list of the Acts of Parliament and regulations which apply in all circumstances, but a summary of those most commonly encountered.

4.2   The Acts of Parliament and regulations referred to in this Section may broadly be seen to affect the building, its site and environment and the safety of working practices on and within the building. In many cases the legislation will be associated with the age and condition of the building and its position in the normal building life-cycle.

LEGISLATION AFFECTING THE BUILDING

The Fire Precautions Act 1971

4.3   The Fire Precautions Act is primarily concerned with the provision and maintenance of safe means of escape in case of fire in buildings. All buildings put to a designated use under the Act are required to have a fire certificate unless they are exempt. Fire certificates are issued by the local fire authority, but the task of carrying out inspections and assessments of premises is delegated to local fire brigades. Fire certificates are only required for premises which are put to certain "designated" uses and to date, only two designating orders have been made covering:

a)   hotels or boarding houses where sleeping accommodation is provided for more than six staff or guests (or some sleeping accommodation is provided above the first floor or below the ground floor), and

b)   factories, offices, shops and railway premises where more than 20 people are at work at any particular time, or more than 10 people work other than on the ground floor.

4.4   Newly erected or altered premises covered by the Building Regulations are dealt with in Section 3, however there may be a case where an existing building is to be put to a designated use where alterations are unnecessary. If it is decided that a fire certificate is needed then application must be made to the fire authority in the prescribed form in accordance with the requirements of Section 5 of the Act.

The Fire Precautions (Workplace) Regulations 1997*

4.5   The Regulations were made to implement the general fire safety provisions of the European Framework and Workplace Directives, which are not specifically dealt with by other legislation. The Regulations impose duties on employers and on others in control of workplaces, with regard to the provision of minimum fire safety standards in places of work. They apply to all workplaces including those covered by other fire specific fire safety legislation (such as those for which a Fire Certificate is in force, or has been applied for under the Fire Precautions Act).

In most cases employers are required to undertake a fire risk assessment of the workplace to establish the level of precautions necessary to ensure the safety of employees in the event of fire. This might entail, for example:

- equipping the workplace with fire fighting equipment and fire detectors and alarms;

- ensuring that fire fighting equipment is easily accessible, simple to use and indicated by appropriate signs;

- making sure that properly trained employees are nominated to implement the necessary fire safety measures;

- making sure that adequate arrangements are made regarding contact with the emergency services;

- providing suitable emergency routes and exits;

- arranging for a system of maintenance to ensure that all equipment is kept in good working order.

It is the duty of every fire authority to enforce the Regulations in their area and they have powers to inspect premises at any time to ensure compliance with the Regulations.

The Building Act 1984

4.6   Those parts of the Building Act which cover the Building Regulations and the linked powers are discussed in Sections 1 to 3 of the Manual. However, there are other parts which may affect your building even if the Regulations do not apply. These are referred to in Part III of the Act (ss 59 to 83) and the most commonly encountered sections cover the powers of the local authority to control:

- dangerous and defective premises, ss 76 to 79;

- the demolition of buildings, ss 80 to 83;

- means of escape in case of fire from certain high buildings, s 72;

---

*   as amended by the Fire Precautions (Workplace) (Amendment) Regulations 1999 SI 1999/1877

- the raising of chimneys if overreached by building work on an adjoining building, s 73;

The London Building Acts 1930 to 1982

4.7   Although much of the content of the London Building Acts was repealed when the Building (Inner London) Regulations 1985 came into force, a number of provisions were retained which apply only to building work in London, and mostly only in Inner London. The most important provisions contained in the London Building Acts (Amendment) Act 1939, are as follows:

- buildings in excess height and cubical content, s 20;

- uniting of buildings, s 21;

- special and temporary buildings and structures, ss 29 to 31;

- means of escape in case of fire in new buildings, s 34;

- means of escape in old buildings, ss 35 to 37;

- dangerous and neglected structures, ss 60 to 70.

These powers are usually administered by the local authority building control department of the relevant London Borough.

Local Acts of Parliament

4.8   Although the Building Act 1984 has rationalised many of the controls over buildings there still exist over 30 local Acts of Parliament which are enforced by local authorities. Local authorities are obliged by section 90 of the Building Act to keep a copy of any local Act provisions and these must be available for public inspection free of charge at all reasonable times.

Since much of this local legislation was enacted to meet local needs and perceived deficiencies in national legislation the provisions of one local Act may be quite different from those of another. An idea of the range and scope of the matters covered by local Acts may be gained from the following list of typical provisions:

- special fire precautions for basement garages or for large garages;

- access for the fire brigade;

- fire precautions in buildings in excess of 18.3 m in height;

- requirements for all buildings to have separate foul and surface water drainage systems;

- controls over the construction of retaining walls;

It will be evident that some of the provisions in the list above are also covered by the Building Regulations. In these cases it will be necessary to satisfy the requirements of both the local act and the Building Regulations, although parts of some local acts defer to corresponding Building Regulations.

The Housing Act 1985

4.9   The provisions of this Act authorise housing authorities to require the carrying out of specified work in order to make houses fit for occupation. An example of the way the Act works is related to the control of houses in multiple occupation (ie those in which the occupants do not form part of a single household). These are covered by sections 345 to 394 of the Act and among other things the housing authority (District Councils or Inner London Boroughs) may require works to be carried out which relate to the provision of:

- storage accommodation;

- facilities for the preparation and cooking of food;

- adequate water closets, baths, showers and hand basins with hot and cold water supplies;

- suitable means of escape in case of fire and other fire precautions.

The Party Wall etc. Act 1996

4.10   The Act provides a framework for preventing and resolving disputes which may arise between neighbouring owners, in relation to the construction and repair of party walls and boundary walls, and excavations near neighbouring buildings. If you intend to carry out work which involves:

- work on an existing wall shared with another property

- building on the boundary with a neighbouring property

- excavating near a neighbouring building

you must give the adjoining owners notice of your intentions in a way set down in the Act. Adjoining owners can agree or disagree with what is proposed (silence is taken as dissent). Where there is a disagreement the Act provides for the resolution of disputes. A free explanatory booklet is available from DTLR (see Section 5).

The Construction Products Regulations 1991

4.11 The Construction Products Regulations, which came into force on 27 December 1991, implement the Construction Products Directive[1], and apply to products produced for incorporation in a permanent manner in construction works.

The Regulations require products to have such characteristics that the works in which they are incorporated can, if properly built, satisfy any essential requirements which apply to the works. Products which bear the CE marking will be presumed to satisfy this requirement, unless there are reasonable grounds for suspecting that this is not the case (e.g. the product has been damaged) or for suspecting that the CE marking has not been affixed in accordance with the provisions of Regulation 5 of the Regulations.

The Regulations were amended in 1994 by the Construction Products (Amendment) Regulations[2].

The Gas Safety (Installation and Use) Regulations 1998

4.12 These Regulations, control the risks associated with the use of gas supplied from gas storage vessels or via mains pipes.

The main purposes of the Regulations are to require:

- that gas work is carried out by a competent person;

- that the employer of the competent person is recognised as being approved by the Health and Safety Executive (at present this means that they must be members of the Council for Registered Gas Installers (CORGI));

- that gas appliances, gas fittings, installation pipework and flues are installed safely and that checks are carried out to ensure compliance with the Regulations;

- that any flue be installed in a safe position;

- that no alterations are carried out to any premises in which a gas fitting or gas storage vessel is fitted which would adversely affect safety or cause non-compliance with the Regulations;

- gas appliances and installation pipework to be maintained in a safe condition in workplaces covered by the Regulations;

- restrictions on the installation of certain types of gas appliances in bathrooms and sleeping accommodation or in cupboards or compartments in such rooms;

- all gas appliances and pipework installed in rented premises to be maintained in a safe condition (including the keeping of maintenance records);

- that LPG storage vessels, and LPG fired appliances fitted with automatic ignition devices or pilot lights are not installed in cellars or basements.

The Disability Discrimination Act 1995

4.13 The Act is aimed at ending the discrimination which many disabled people face in the areas of employment, the provision of goods, facilities and services, and in the buying or renting of land or property.

The first rights under Part III of the Act came into force on 2 December 1996 and placed duties on those providing goods, facilities and services:

- not to refuse service;

- not to provide a worse standard of service; and

- not to offer service on worse terms.

From 1 October 1999, it has been necessary for service providers to:

- take reasonable steps to change practices, policies and procedures which make it impossible or unreasonably difficult for disabled people to use a service;

- provide auxiliary aids or services which would enable disabled people to use a service; and

- overcome physical barriers by providing a service by a reasonable alternative method.

From 2004, service providers will have to take reasonable steps to remove, alter, or provide reasonable means of avoiding physical features that make it impossible or unreasonably difficult for disabled people to use a service.

The Building (Local Authority Charges) Regulations 1998

4.14 The above 'Charges Regulations' replaced the Building (Prescribed Fees) Regulations 1994 and came into force on 1 April 1999. The regulations (which do not apply to approved inspectors) require each local authority to fix its own charges within a scheme for carrying out its building control functions according to principles, as prescribed

1 Council Directive 89/106/EEC of 21 December 1988, OJ L40/12 of 11 February 1989
2 SI 1994, No. 3051

in the regulations. This includes the principle that the income derived from those charges over a continuous/rolling period of three years is not less than the cost directly or indirectly incurred - i.e. full cost recovery. The five prescribed functions for which a local authority must fix charges in their scheme are:

- A plan charge for the passing or rejection of plans of proposed building work deposited with the local authority (payable on deposit).

- An inspection charge for the inspection of work in progress (payable after the first inspection - although local authorities have discretion not to request this charge in prescribed 'de minimus' circumstances).

- A building notice charge when the building notice procedure is used (the charge must be the sum of the local authority's plan and inspection charges and is payable when the building notice is given to the authority).

- A reversion charge where an approved inspector is the building control body and the initial notice is cancelled so that control reverts to the local authority (the charge must equal the charge for a building notice and is payable on the first occasion that the relevant plans are inspected).

- A regularisation charge for applications relating to unauthorised building work (the charge must be 20% greater than the charge for a building notice and is payable at the time of application).

The Charges Regulations contain two key principles for charging. For work comprising:

- the erection of small domestic buildings (up to 300m² in floor area and up to three storeys), or

- small detached garages and carports with floor area up to 40m², or

- domestic extensions (including associated access work) with floor area up to 60m² (for the erection of a number of extensions to a building their floor areas must be aggregated),

it must be fixed by reference to the floor area of the building or extension concerned.

The charges for all other types of work must be fixed according to an estimate of the cost of the building work.

The following provisions in the Charges Regulations should also be noted:

- Where the proper costs of a local authority do not exceed £450,000 over the three year period or where at least 65% of the charges income is derived from building

work involving small domestic buildings such as extensions, garages and carports, the income derived should cover at least 90% of costs (i.e. not full cost recovery).

- Local authorities must prepare an annual building control statement setting out their income and costs (which is subject to external audit review).

- Local authorities may not charge for building work which comprises the installation of cavity fill material or the installation of unvented hot water systems in prescribed circumstances.

- Reduced charges may be fixed for repetitive building work or applications/notices for substantially the same work, as prescribed.

- Local authorities may not charge in relation to the control of prescribed types of building work which is solely for the benefit of disabled people.

- Charges for work may be paid in instalments, with the agreement of the local authority.

- Local authorities must refund any plan charge if they do not give notice of passing or rejection of plans within the 'relevant period' required by section 16 of the Building Act 1984.

- Before bringing a charges scheme into effect, or making any amendments to it, local authorities must publicise it giving at least 7 days notice, and must also make the scheme available for inspection free of charge.

LEGISLATION AFFECTING THE SITE AND ENVIRONMENT OF THE BUILDING

The Highways Act 1980

4.15 This Act is mainly concerned with the creation of highways and with the rights and duties of people who use them, and the powers of the authorities who control them. In most cases the controlling authority will be the county council (borough council in Greater London) except for trunk roads which are the responsibility of the DTLR (Highways Agency).

Those sections where building work most often affects a highway are as follows:

- control and removal of builder's skips, ss 139, 140;

- dangerous land adjoining a highway, s 165;

- building operations affecting public safety, s 168;

- control of scaffolding on highways, s 169;

- control of mixing of mortar etc highways, s 170;

- control of deposit of building materials, rubbish, etc., and making temporary excavations in streets maintainable at the public expense, s 171;

- hoardings to be set up and securely erected during building, ss 172,173;

- construction of buildings over a highway, ss 176 to 178;

- construction of cellars under streets, ss 179, 180;

- vehicular or pedestrian access to premises necessitating the construction of a carriage crossing, s 184.

The Water Industry Act 1991

4.16 The responsibilities of the water undertakers regarding sewers, drains, discharges and drinking water are now principally to be found in the Water Industry Act 1991. The sections with most relevance to building work are:

- duty of sewerage undertaker to provide a system of public sewers, s 94;

- rights of owners and occupiers of premises to connect to a public sewer, ss 106 to 108;

- duty to supply water for domestic purposes, s 52;

- supply of water for non-domestic premises, s 55;

Water fittings which are installed and used in premises to which water is supplied by a water undertaker are controlled by the Water Supply (Water Fittings) Regulations 1999 made under s 74 of the Water Industry Act.

The Clean Air Acts 1956 and 1993

4.17 The Clean Air Acts are the principal measures dealing with atmospheric pollution from furnaces and heating plant. From the viewpoint of building work, local authorities are empowered to control, among other things, the height of chimneys for furnaces, and the choice of fuels that can be combusted.

The Environmental Protection Act 1990

4.18 In terms of its application to buildings, the Environmental Protection Act (as amended by the Environment Act 1995) is the principal measure dealing with the collection and disposal of waste. Section 45 of the 1990 Act places a duty on waste collection authorities (primarily District Councils and London Boroughs) to collect all household waste in their areas. (Exceptions are made for isolated parts where other adequate disposal

arrangements have been made). They must collect commercial waste if requested to do so by the occupier of the premises and they may make a charge. They are under no obligation to collect industrial waste but may do so with the consent of the relevant waste disposal authority, and they may charge for this service also.

These powers and duties may affect building work in that the waste disposal authorities may under sections 46 and 47 require the provision of suitable waste receptacles for household, commercial or industrial waste.

LEGISLATION AFFECTING THE SAFETY OF WORKING PRACTICES ON AND WITHIN THE BUILDING.

The Health and Safety at Work etc. Act 1974

4.19 The main purpose of the Act is to secure the health, safety and welfare of people at work and of others whose health and safety may be affected by work activities. The Act sets out general requirements for health and safety at work and its provisions have been supplemented with detailed regulations to deal with particular situations and practices at work. Those which most affect building operations are set out below. The Act is enforced by the Health and Safety Executive although much of its work (involving non hazardous operations) is carried out by local authorities.

The Workplace (Health, Safety and Welfare) Regulations 1992

4.20 The Regulations were made under the Health and Safety at Work etc. Act 1974 and implement provisions of Workplace Directive 89/654/EEC. A general duty is placed on employers to ensure that workplaces comply with the requirements of the Regulations which include provisions for ventilation, temperature control, lighting levels, cleanliness, adequacy of room dimensions, safe use of windows and doors etc., sanitary conveniences and washing facilities. The Regulations apply to workplaces in use.

New buildings erected under the Building Regulations and which follow the guidance in the Approved Documents will, in most cases satisfy the requirements of the Workplace Regulations regarding the provision of ventilation, sanitary conveniences and washing facilities, permanent stairs, ladders and ramps, provision of guarding to prevent falls, the safe use of doors, and the safe use and cleaning of windows.

The Construction (Design and Management) Regulations 1994

4.21 The Construction (Design and Management) Regulations 1994 place duties upon clients, client's agents (where appointed), designers, and contractors, to rethink their approach to health and safety so that it is taken into account and then co-ordinated and managed effectively throughout all stages of construction and demolition. The Regulations were made under the Health and Safety at Work etc. Act 1974 and implement provisions of Directive No. 89/654/EEC. The Regulations apply to construction work, in a broad sense, and related activities. An important feature is a duty on the client to appoint a planning supervisor, who is responsible for a pre-tender health and safety plan and the preparation and adherence to a health and safety plan for the project. The Regulations do not normally apply to householders having work carried out to their own residences, or to specified small construction works.

The Construction (Health, Safety and Welfare) Regulations 1996

4.22 The Regulations were made under the Health and Safety at Work etc. Act 1974 to implement Directive No. 92/57/EEC on minimum health and safety requirements for temporary or mobile construction sites for building, civil engineering or engineering construction. The Regulations impose general duties on employers, the self-employed and others who control the way work is carried out and on employees with regard to their own actions. They are enforced by the Health and Safety Executive.

More specifically, requirements are imposed with regard to the provision of:

- safe work places (ie access and egress, suitable and sufficient working space etc);
- measures to prevent falls (including falls through fragile materials);
- stability of structures;
- measures to ensure safe means of demolition or dismantling;
- safety of excavations;
- safe traffic routes about the site;
- measures to ensure that doors and gates have safety devices;
- measures to reduce the risk of fire, and the provision of fire detection and fire fighting equipment;
- emergency escape routes;
- welfare facilities such as sanitary conveniences, washing facilities, drinking water, rest areas etc.

Section 5

SECTION 5 – SUPPORTING DOCUMENTS AND INFORMATION

The following legislation and guidance documents are published by HMSO or the Stationery Office unless otherwise indicated.

5.1 Principal Legislation

The Building Act 1984, Chapter 55 (as amended)

The Building Regulations 2000, S. I. 2000 No. 2531 as amended by:

The Building (Amendment) Regulations 2001, S.I 2001 No. 3335

The Building (Approved Inspectors etc.) Regulations 2000, S.I 2000 No. 2532 as amended by:

The Building (Approved Inspectors etc.) (Amendment) Regulations 2001, S.I 2001 No. 3336

The Building (Local Authority Charges) Regulations 1998, S.I. 1998 No. 3129

5.2 Additional Legislation

The Fire Precautions Act 1971, Chapter 40 as amended

The Fire Precautions (Workplace) Regulations 1997, S.I. 1997 No.1840 as amended by:

The Fire Precautions (Workplace) (Amendment) Regulations 1999, S.I. 1999 No.1877

The London Building Acts 1939 to 1982

The Housing Act 1985, Chapter 68 as amended

The Party Wall etc. Act 1996[1]

The Construction Products Regulations 1991, S.I. 1991, No. 1620

The Gas Safety (Installation and Use) Regulations 1998, S.I. 1998, No. 2451

The Disability Discrimination Act 1995, Chapter 50

The Highways Act 1980, Chapter 66 as amended

The Water Industry Act 1991, Chapter 56 as amended

The Clean Air Acts 1956 and 1993

The Environmental Protection Act 1990, Chapter 43 as amended

The Health and Safety at Work etc. Act 1974, Chapter 37 as amended

The Workplace (Health, Safety and Welfare) Regulations 1992.

The Construction (Design and Management) Regulations 1994, S.I. 1994 No.3140 as amended by:

The Construction (Design and Management)(Amendment) Regulations 2000, S.I. 2000 No.2380

The Construction (Health Safety and Welfare) Regulations 1996, S.I. 1996 No. 1592

5.3 Guidance Documents

Approved Document to support regulation 7, *Materials and workmanship:* 1999 Edition, amended 2000

Approved Document A – *Structure*: 1992 Edition, fourth impression (with amendments) 1994, further amended 2000 (under review)

Approved Document B – *Fire safety*: 2000 Edition, amended 2000

Approved Document C – *Site preparation and resistance to moisture*: 1992 Edition, second impression (with amendments) 1992, further amended 2000 (under review)

Approved Document D – *Toxic substances*: amended 1992, further amended 2000

Approved Document E – *Resistance to the passage of sound*: 1992 Edition, second impression (with amendments) 1992, further amended 2000 (under review)

Approved Document F – *Ventilation*: 1995 Edition, amended 2000

Approved Document G – *Hygiene*: 1992 Edition, second impression (with amendments) 1992, further amended 2000

Approved Document H – *Drainage and waste disposal*: 2002 Edition

Approved Document J – *Combustion appliances and fuel storage systems*: 2002 Edition

Approved Document K – *Protection from falling, collision and impact*: 1998 Edition, amended 2000

Approved Document L1 – *Conservation of fuel and power in dwellings*: 2002 Edition

Approved Document L2 – *Conservation of fuel and power in buildings other than dwellings*: 2002 Edition

Approved Document M – *Access and facilities for disabled people*: 1999 Edition, amended 2000 (under review)

Approved Document N – *Glazing – safety in relation to impact, opening and cleaning*: 1998 Edition, amended 2000

---

1 Copies of a free booklet may be obtained from DLTR free literature, PO Box 236, Wetherby, West Yorkshire, LS23 7NB. Telephone: 0870 1226 236

SUPPORTING DOCUMENTS AND INFORMATION

Approved Document, *Timber intermediate floors for dwellings (excluding compartment floors)*, TRADA 1996, Published by Timber Research and Development Association, Stocking Lane, Hughenden Valley, High Wycombe, Buckinghamshire, HP14 4ND.

Approved Document, *Basements for dwellings*, 1997 Published by British Cement Association, Century House, Telford Avenue, Crowthorne, Berkshire, RG45 6YS.

5.4 Determinations and Appeals

Applications for determination, and appeals to the Secretary of State against refusal by a local authority to relax or dispense with a requirement in Schedule 1 of the Building Regulations 2000 (as amended) should, in England, be addressed to:

> Building Regulations Division
> Department for Transport, Local Government and the Regions
> Zone 3/C1
> Eland House
> Bressenden Place
> London SW1E 5DU

and in Wales to:

> Housing Division
> National Assembly for Wales
> Crown Buildings, Cathays Park
> Cardiff CF1 3NQ

A Guide to Determinations and Appeals, 2001, published jointly by the DTLR/NAW - copies available from:

> DTLR Free Literature
> PO Box 236
> Wetherby
> West Yorkshire
> LS23 7NB
> Telephone: 0870 1226 236
> Email: dtlr@twoten.press.net

5.5 Approved Inspectors

Further information on corporate and non-corporate Approved Inspectors

Inspectors operating in your area may be obtained from:

> The Association of Consultant Approved Inspectors,
> Lutyens House
> Billing Brook Road
> Weston Favell
> Northampton
> NN3 8NW
> Telephone: 01435 862487

or the website: http://www.acai.org.uk

5.6 Local Authority

Further information on local authority building control is available from:

> Building Control
> LABC Services
> 137 Lupus Street
> London
> SW1V 3HE
> Telephone: 020 7641 8737